Cuba desse

With 500 recipes, Dulces de Cuba is a sweet trip through Cuban food.

Donnie C. South

Table of Content

Tres Leches Cake: 20
    Instructions: 21

Flan de Coco (Coconut Flan): 22
    Instructions: 23

Arroz con Leche (Rice Pudding): 24
    Instructions: 25

Churros Cubanos: 26
    Instructions: 26

Coconut Flan: 27
    Instructions: 28

Mantecado Ice Cream: 29
    Instructions: 29

Buñuelos de Viento (Wind Fritters): 30
    Instructions: 31

Dulce de Leche Cheesecake: 32
    Instructions: 32

Turrones de Maní (Peanut Brittle): 33

Instructions: 34

Crema de Vie: 35

Instructions: 35

Plátanos en Tentación (Caramelized Plantains): 36

Instructions: 36

Cuban Chocolate Pots de Crème: 37

Instructions: 37

Merenguitos (Meringue Cookies): 38

Instructions: 38

Cinnamon Sugar Churro Bites: 39

Instructions: 39

Guava and Cheese Empanadas: 40

Instructions: 40

Cuban Rice Pudding Flan (Flan de Arroz con Leche): 41

Instructions: 42

Cuban Guava Bars: 43

Instructions: 43

Torrejas (Cuban-Style French Toast): 44

Instructions: 45

Arroz con Maíz (Cuban Sweet Corn Rice): 45

Instructions: 46

Coconut Flan: 47

Instructions: 47

3 | Page

Mango Sorbet: 48

    Instructions: 48

Pastel de Malanga (Malanga Cake): 49

    Instructions: 49

Mantecados (Cuban Shortbread Cookies): 50

    Instructions: 50

Guava Pastries (Pastelitos de Guayaba): 51

    Instructions: 51

Mango Tres Leches Cake: 52

    Instructions: 52

Guanábana Ice Cream: 53

    Instructions: 53

Café Cubano Affogato: 54

    Instructions: 54

Pineapple Empanadas: 55

    Instructions: 55

Guava Mousse: 55

    uctions: 56

Quesillo (Cuban Flan): 56

    Instruction 57

Plátanos Maduros Fritos (Fried Sweet Plantains): 57

    Instructions: 58

Chocolate Turrón: 58

    Instructions: 58

Guava and Cream Cheese Tart: 59

    Instructions: 60

Cuban Coffee Panna Cotta: 61

    Instructions: 61

Arroz con Dulce (Cuban Rice Pudding): 62

    Instructions: 62

Coconut Rice Pudding: 63

    Instructions: 63

Guava and Cream Cheese Pastries: 64

    Instructions: 64

Guava and Cheese Flan: 65

    Instructions: 65

Caramelized Pineapple with Rum Sauce: 66

    Instructions: 67

Cuban Chocolate Truffles: 67

    Instructions: 68

Chocolate Coconut Bars: 68

    Instructions: 69

Guava Ice Cream: 69

    Instructions: 70

Torrejas de Calabaza (Pumpkin French Toast): 70

    Instructions: 71

Mango Coconut Rice Pudding: 71

    Instructions: 71

Cinnamon Sugar Plantain Chips: 72
    Instructions: 72

Guava Custard: 73
    Instructions: 73

Guava and Cheese Turnovers: 74
    Instructions: 74

Banana Fritters (Buñuelos de Plátano): 75
    Instructions: 75

Coconut Rum Balls: 76
    Instructions: 76

Papaya Sorbet: 77
    Instructions: 77

Cuban Chocolate Fondue: 78
    Instructions: 78

Guava and Cream Cheese Cupcakes: 78
    Instructions: 79

Taro Root Pudding (Pudin de Malanga): 80
    Instructions: 81

Caramel Flan Cake: 81
    Instructions: 82

Guava and Cheese Croissants: 83
    Instructions: 83

Guava and Cheese Pancakes: 84
    Instructions: 84

Coconut Rice Cake: 85
    Instructions: 85

Pineapple Sorbet: 86
    Instructions: 86

Coconut Rum Cake: 87
    Instructions: 87

Mamey Ice Cream: 88
    Instructions: 89

Coconut Custard Pie: 89
    Instructions: 89

Plantain Pudding (Pudín de Plátano): 90
    Instructions: 91

Guava and Cream Cheese Brownies: 91
    Instructions: 92

Cuban Coffee Ice Cream: 93
    Instructions: 93

Cinnamon Sugar Churro Waffles: 94
    Instructions: 95

Coconut Macaroons: 95
    Instructions: 96

Guava Swirl Cheesecake: 97
    Instructions: 97

Pineapple Upside-Down Cake: 98
    Instructions: 99

Cuban Bread Pudding (Pudin de Pan): 100

    Instructions: 100

Cocada Cubana (Cuban Coconut Candy): 101

    Instructions: 101

Chocolate Babka with Rum Glaze: 102

    Instructions: 103

Guava and Cheese Stuffed French Toast: 104

    Instructions: 105

Mango Coconut Popsicles: 105

    Instructions: 106

Caramelized Plantain Cake: 106

    Instructions: 107

Cuban Coffee Chocolate Mousse: 107

    Instructions: 108

Guava and Cream Cheese Oat Bars: 108

    Instructions: 109

Tamarind Sorbet: 110

    Instructions: 110

Coconut Bread Pudding: 111

    Instructions: 111

Chocolate Coconut Rice Pudding: 112

    Instructions: 112

Guava and Cheese Quesadillas: 113

    Instructions: 113

Cuban Chocolate Tiramisu: 114

    Instructions: 114

Pineapple Coconut Tres Leches Cake: 115

    Instructions: 116

Plantain Fritters with Guava Dipping Sauce: 117

    Instructions: 118

Caramelized Banana Crepes: 118

    Instructions: 119

Guava and Cheese Muffins: 120

    Instructions: 120

Coconut Custard Flan: 121

    Instructions: 121

Chocolate Coconut Cupcakes: 123

    Instructions: 123

Guava and Cream Cheese Empanadas: 124

    Instructions: 125

Guava and Cheese Danish: 126

    Instructions: 127

Pineapple Rum Cake: 128

    Instructions: 128

Coconut Panna Cotta: 129

    Instructions: 130

Mamey Smoothie Bowl: 130

    Instructions: 131

Guava and Cream Cheese Scones: **131**
    Instructions: 132

Cuban Coffee Chocolate Chip Cookies: **133**
    Instructions: 133

Plantain and Coconut Tarts: **134**
    Instructions: 134

Guava and Cheese Stuffed Crepes: **136**
    Instructions: 136

Caramelized Mango with Coconut Cream: **137**
    Instructions: 137

Chocolate Coconut Mousse: **138**
    Instructions: 138

Guava and Cream Cheese Parfait: **139**
    Instructions: 140

Pineapple Coconut Macadamia Nut Bars: **140**
    Instructions: 141

Tres Leches Flan: **141**
    Instructions: 142

Guava and Cheese Palmiers: **143**
    Instructions: 143

Coconut Rum Trifle: **144**
    Instructions: 144

Cinnamon Sugar Plantain Empanadas: **145**
    Instructions: 145

Mamey Cheesecake: 147
    Instructions: 147

Guava and Cheese Stuffed Waffles: 148
    Instructions: 149

Banana and Coconut Bread: 150
    Instructions: 150

Caramelized Papaya with Rum Glaze: 151
    Instructions: 151

Cuban Coffee Tres Leches Cake: 152
    Instructions: 153

Pineapple Coconut Cupcakes: 154
    Instructions: 154

Mamey and Coconut Smoothie: 156
    Instructions: 156

Guava and Cheese Brioche: 156
    Instructions: 157

Chocolate Coconut Biscotti: 158
    Instructions: 158
    Instructions: 160

Guava and Cream Cheese Cinnamon Rolls: 161
    Instructions: 161

Coconut Cream Puffs: 163
    Instructions: 163

Caramelized Guava with Whipped Cream: 165

Instructions: 165

Guava and Cheese Stuffed Pancakes: 166

Instructions: 166

Pineapple Coconut Tart: 167

Instructions: 168

Cuban Coffee Mousse Cake: 169

Instructions: 170

Chocolate Coconut Rice Krispie Treats: 171

Instructions: 171

Mango and Coconut Scones: 172

Instructions: 172

Guava and Cheese Stuffed Donuts: 173

Instructions: 174

Taro Root and Coconut Tapioca Pudding: 176

Instructions: 176

Coconut Almond Joy Bars: 177

Instructions: 177

Caramelized Banana Bread Pudding: 178

Instructions: 178

Guava and Cream Cheese Bread: 179

Instructions: 180

Cuban Coffee Tiramisu Cake: 180

Instructions: 181

- Pineapple Coconut Muffins: ... 182
  - Instructions: ... 182
- Mamey and Coconut Panna Cotta: ... 183
  - Instructions: ... 183
- Guava and Cheese Stuffed Biscuits: ... 185
  - Instructions: ... 185
- Chocolate Coconut Brownie Bites: ... 186
  - Instructions: ... 187
- Coconut Tres Leches Flan: ... 188
  - Instructions: ... 188
- Taro Root and Coconut Pancakes: ... 189
  - Instructions: ... 190
- Guava and Cream Cheese Twists: ... 191
  - Instructions: ... 191
- Coconut Key Lime Pie: ... 192
  - Instructions: ... 192
- Caramelized Plantain Mousse: ... 193
  - Instructions: ... 194
- Cuban Coffee Éclairs: ... 195
  - Instructions: ... 195
- Pineapple Coconut Bread Pudding: ... 197
  - Instructions: ... 197
- Guava and Cheese Stuffed Croissant Donuts: ... 198
  - Instructions: ... 199

Chocolate Coconut Chia Pudding: **199**
    Instructions: 200

Coconut Pecan Pie: **200**
    Instructions: 201

Tres Leches Ice Cream Cake: **202**
    Instructions: 202

Guava and Cream Cheese Popsicles: **203**
    Instructions: 203

Mamey and Coconut Cheesecake Bars: **204**
    Instructions: 204

Guava and Cheese Stuffed Beignets: **205**
    Instructions: 206

Pineapple Coconut Rice Krispie Treats: **207**
    Instructions: 207

Caramelized Mango Sorbet: **208**
    Instructions: 208

Cuban Coffee Brownie Trifle: **209**
    Instructions: 209

Chocolate Coconut Mochi: **210**
    Instructions: 211

Coconut Lime Bars: **211**
    Instructions: 212

Taro Root and Coconut Cupcakes: **213**
    Instructions: 214

Guava and Cream Cheese French Toast Casserole: 215

    Instructions: 215

Guava and Cheese Ice Cream: 216

    Instructions: 216

Pineapple Coconut Chocolate Fondue: 217

    Instructions: 217

Mamey and Coconut Tres Leches Cake: 218

    Instructions: 219

Guava and Cheese Stuffed Cinnamon Sugar Pretzels: 220

    Instructions: 220

Coconut Almond Joy Bars: 222

    Instructions: 222

Caramelized Banana Split: 223

    Instructions: 223

Cuban Coffee Tres Leches Flan: 224

    Instructions: 224

Taro Root and Coconut Popsicles: 226

    Instructions: 226

Guava and Cheese Stuffed Monkey Bread: 226

    Instructions: 227

Pineapple Coconut Crepe Cake: 228

    Instructions: 229

Coconut Tapioca Pearls: 230

    Instructions: 230

Tres Leches Bread Pudding: **231**
    Instructions: 231

Guava and Cream Cheese Danishes: **232**
    Instructions: 232

Mamey and Coconut Mousse: **233**
    Instructions: 233

Cuban Coffee Macarons: **234**
    Instructions: 235

Chocolate Coconut Crepes: **236**
    Instructions: 236

Coconut Banana Bread Pudding: **237**
    Instructions: 238

Caramelized Plantain Ice Cream: **238**
    Instructions: 239

Guava and Cheese Stuffed Waffle Cones: **239**
    Instructions: 240

Pineapple Coconut Whoopie Pies: **241**
    Instructions: 241

Taro Root and Coconut Brownies: **242**
    Instructions: 243

Guava and Cream Cheese Stuffed Chocolate Truffles: **244**
    Instructions: 244

Coconut Mango Rice Pudding: **245**
    Instructions: 245

Tres Leches Cupcakes: **246**

    Instructions: 246

Mamey and Coconut Chia Parfait: **248**

    Instructions: 248

Cuban Coffee and Chocolate Fondue: **249**

    Instructions: 249

Guava and Cheese Stuffed Pop Tarts: **249**

    Instructions: 250

Pineapple Coconut Oatmeal Bars: **251**

    Instructions: 252

Coconut Tiramisu: **253**

    Instructions: 253

Caramelized Banana Foster: **254**

    Instructions: 254

Chocolate Coconut Cream Pie: **255**

    Instructions: 255

Taro Root and Coconut Macarons: **256**

    Instructions: 257

Guava and Cream Cheese Stuffed Babka: **258**

    Instructions: 259

Cuban Coffee Ice Cream Sandwiches: **260**

    Instructions: 261

Pineapple Coconut Creme Brulee: **262**

    Instructions: 263

Guava and Cheese Stuffed Cookie Sandwiches: 264

    Instructions: 264

Coconut Key Lime Tartlets: 265

    Instructions: 266

Tres Leches Tiramisu Trifles: 267

    Instructions: 268

    Conclusion *269*

Introduction:

FLAVORS OF THE TROPICS: A JOURNEY THROUGH CUBAN DESSERTS

Here's a trip through the heart of Cuba's food culture, where sugar, spice, and all the good things in the world come together to make the island's tastiest treats. Please discover this book's wide range of delicious Cuban treats, from well-known favorites like Tres Leches Cake to lesser-known gems like Guava Pastries. Get ready to taste Cuba's sweet side!

INDULGE IN THE SWEET TRADITIONS OF CUBA

Cuba is known for its lively music, food, and culture; its sweets are no different. Come with us as we learn about Cuban families' sweet practices for many years. From the sweet smell of freshly brewed Cuban coffee to the allure of flan, our guide takes you on a journey through sugar that you will never forget.

CUBA: WHERE EVERY MEAL ENDS WITH A SWEET NOTE

For Cubans, a meal is only complete with something sweet at the end. This guide will help you find the delicious sweets that finish a Cuban meal. From Havana's busy streets to Varadero's quiet beaches, we've compiled a list of must-try desserts. Get ready to make Cuban food in your own home!

SABOR CUBANO: A DESSERT ODYSSEY

Get ready to go on a trip to the center of Cuba's dessert culture, where old practices meet new ideas in the world of sweets. From the simple Arroz con Leche to the complex Cuban Rum Cake, "Sabor Cubano" lets you discover the island's sweetest secrets. Come with us as we learn about the stories, flavors, and methods that make delicious Cuban desserts.

CUBA'S SWEET SYMPHONY: A DESSERT COOKBOOK

In Cuban food full of rhythm and color, sweets are the crescendo that stays with you. The book "Cuba's Sweet Symphony" tells you about the flavors, textures, and stories that make up Cuban sweets. Get ready to dance to the sweet sounds of Cuban food culture, from the sour Mojito Pie to the smooth Chocolate Turrón.

TRES LECHES CAKE:

INGREDIENTS:

- 1 cup all-purpose flour
- 1 1/2 tsp baking powder
- 1/4 tsp salt
- 1/2 cup unsalted butter
- 1 cup granulated sugar
- 5 large eggs
- 1 tsp vanilla extract
- 1 can (14 oz) sweetened condensed milk
- 1 can (12 oz) evaporated milk
- 1 cup whole milk
- 1 cup heavy cream
- Whipped cream and fresh berries for garnish (optional)

Instructions:

1. Warm the oven up to 175°F (350°F). A 9x13-inch baking dish should be greased and floured.
2. Mix the flour, baking powder, and salt in a bowl with a whisk.
3. Add the butter and 1 cup of powdered sugar to a different bowl. Beat them together until they are light and fluffy.
4. Add the eggs and beat well after each one one at a time. Add the vanilla extract and mix well.
5. Slowly add the dry ingredients to the wet ones until they are mixed.
6. Put the batter into the baking dish that has been prepared. Bake for 30 to 35 minutes or until a toothpick stuck in the middle comes out clean.
7. Mix the evaporated milk, whole milk, heavy cream, and sweetened condensed milk in a different bowl while baking the cake.
8. Use a fork to make holes all over the top of the cake while it is still warm after baking.
9. Pour the milk mixture over the cake slowly, ensuring it covers the whole thing.
10. Once the cake is cool enough to touch, please put it in the fridge for at least 4 hours or overnight.
11. If you want, you can serve it cold with whipped cream and fresh berries on top.

FLAN DE COCO (COCONUT FLAN):

INGREDIENTS:

- 1 cup granulated sugar
- 1 can (14 oz) sweetened condensed milk
- 1 can (12 oz) evaporated milk
- 1 can (13.5 oz) coconut milk
- 4 large eggs
- 1 tsp vanilla extract
- 1/4 cup shredded coconut (optional, for garnish)

Instructions:

1. Warm the oven up to 175°F (350°F).
2. Melt the powdered sugar in a saucepan over medium-low heat, stirring all the time, until it turns into caramel. Watch out not to burn it.
3. Quickly pour the caramel into a round 9-inch baking dish and swirl it around to cover the bottom evenly. Leave it alone to harden and cool down.
4. The evaporated milk, sweetened condensed milk, eggs, and vanilla extract should all be put into a blender. Mix until it's smooth.
5. Put the milk mixture into the baking dish covered in caramel.
6. Place the baking dish in a bigger oven-safe pan that is half-filled with hot water. Cover the baking dish with aluminum foil and set it in the pan.
7. Put the flan in an oven that has already been warm and bake it for about an hour, or until it is set but still has a little give in the middle.
8. Take it out of the oven and let it cool down until it's even.
9. Please put it in the fridge for at least four hours or overnight.

10. Run a knife around the edge of the flan to serve, then flip it over onto a serving plate. If you want, you can decorate with shredded coconut.

ARROZ CON LECHE (RICE PUDDING):

INGREDIENTS:

- 1 cup long-grain white rice
- 4 cups whole milk
- 1 cup granulated sugar
- 1 cinnamon stick
- 1 tsp vanilla extract
- 1/2 cup raisins (optional)
- Ground cinnamon for garnish

Instructions:

1. Run cold water over the rice until the water runs clear, then drain.
2. Put the rice, milk, sugar, and cinnamon stick in a big saucepan.
3. Over medium-high heat, bring the mixture to a boil. Then, lower the heat to low and simmer, stirring often, for 20 to 25 minutes, or until the rice is soft and the sauce thickens.
4. After taking out the cinnamon stick, add the vanilla extract and raisins (if using) and mix them in.
5. Place the rice pudding in bowls to serve and top with cinnamon powder.
6. Serve hot or cold

CHURROS CUBANOS:

INGREDIENTS:

- 1 cup water
- 2 1/2 tbsp granulated sugar
- 1/2 tsp salt
- 2 tbsp vegetable oil
- 1 cup all-purpose flour
- 2 quarts vegetable oil for frying
- 1/2 cup granulated sugar (for coating)
- 1 tsp ground cinnamon (for coating)

Instructions:

1. Fill a pot with water. Add salt, 2 1/2 tablespoons of sugar, and 2 tablespoons of vegetable oil. Bring up the temperature.
2. Take it off the heat and add the flour. Mix it in until it makes a dough ball.
3. Heat the 2 quarts of vegetable oil to 375°F (190°C) in a deep fryer or big pot.
4. Put the dough in a pastry bag that has a star-shaped tip.
5. As you cut the dough into 6-inch strips, you can put them into the hot oil.
6. Take the churros out of the oil when they turn golden brown. Use a forked spoon to take them out and let them drain on paper towels.
7. Mix the rest of the sugar and ground cinnamon in a small dish.

8. Cover the warm churros with the cinnamon-sugar mix by rolling them in it.
9. Serve right away.

COCONUT FLAN:

INGREDIENTS:

- 1 cup granulated sugar
- 1 can (14 oz) sweetened condensed milk
- 1 can (12 oz) evaporated milk
- 1 can (13.5 oz) coconut milk
- 4 large eggs
- 1 tsp vanilla extract
- 1/4 cup shredded coconut (optional, for garnish)

Instructions:

1. Warm the oven up to 175°F (350°F).
2. Melt the powdered sugar in a saucepan over medium-low heat, stirring all the time, until it turns into caramel. Watch out not to burn it.
3. Quickly pour the caramel into a round 9-inch baking dish and swirl it around to cover the bottom evenly. Leave it alone to harden and cool down.
4. The evaporated milk, sweetened condensed milk, eggs, and vanilla extract should all be put into a blender. Mix until it's smooth.
5. Put the milk mixture into the baking dish covered in caramel.

6. Place the baking dish in a bigger oven-safe pan that is half-filled with hot water. Cover the baking dish with aluminum foil and set it in the pan.
7. Put the flan in an oven that has already been warm and bake it for about an hour, or until it is set but still has a little give in the middle.
8. Take it out of the oven and let it cool down until it's even.
9. Please put it in the fridge for at least four hours or overnight.
10. Run a knife around the edge of the flan to serve, then flip it over onto a serving plate. If you want, you can decorate with shredded coconu

MANTECADO ICE CREAM:

INGREDIENTS:

- 2 cups heavy cream
- 1 cup whole milk
- 1 cup granulated sugar
- 1 tsp vanilla extract
- 1/4 tsp salt

Instructions:

1. With a whisk, mix the heavy cream, whole milk, sugar, vanilla extract, and salt in a bowl until the sugar is thoroughly mixed in.
2. Put the liquid into an ice cream maker and churn it as directed by the maker's maker.

3. Once the ice cream is smooth, put it in a container that won't let air in. Freeze it for a few hours or until it is hard.
4. You can use cups or cones to serve the Mantecado ice cream.

BUÑUELOS DE VIENTO (WIND FRITTERS):

INGREDIENTS:

- 1 cup water
- 1/4 cup unsalted butter
- 1 cup all-purpose flour
- 1/4 tsp salt
- 4 large eggs
- Vegetable oil for frying
- Powdered sugar for dusting

Instructions:

1. Bring the butter and water to a boil in a pot.
2. All at once, add the flour and salt and stir the mixture well until it makes a smooth ball of dough that pulls away from the pan's sides.
3. Take it off the heat and let it cool down for a while.
4. One at a time, add the eggs and mix well after each one until the dough is smooth and shiny.
5. In a deep fryer or big pot, heat the vegetable oil to 375°F (190°C).

6. Spoons of dough should be dropped into hot oil and fried until they turn golden brown and puff up.
7. Use a slotted spoon to take them out and let them drain on paper towels.
8. Before you serve the Buñuelos de Viento, sprinkle them with powdered sugar.

DULCE DE LECHE CHEESECAKE:

INGREDIENTS:

- 1 1/2 cups graham cracker crumbs
- 1/4 cup granulated sugar
- 1/2 cup unsalted butter, melted
- 3 (8 oz) packages of cream cheese, softened
- 1 cup granulated sugar
- 1 tsp vanilla extract
- 3 large eggs
- 1 cup dulce de leche (homemade or store-bought)

Instructions:

1. Warm the oven up to 160°C (325°F). Clean and grease a 9-inch springform pan.
2. Put the graham cracker crumbs, 1/4 cup of powdered sugar, and melted butter in a bowl and mix them. Fill the pan with the mixture and press it into the bottom.
3. Beat the cream cheese in a different bowl until it's smooth.

4. Add vanilla extract and 1 cup of white sugar. Beat until everything is well mixed.
5. Add the eggs and mix after each one at a time until they are combined.
6. Spread half of the cream cheese mix over the pan's crust.
7. Put small balls of dulce de leche on the cream cheese layer.
8. Add the rest of the cream cheese mixture on top.
9. Mix the dulce de leche into the cheesecake batter with a knife.
10. After the oven is hot, bake the dish for fifty to sixty minutes or until the edges are set, and the middle is still wobbly.
11. Close the oven door a little, leaving the cheesecake there for an hour to cool.
12. Take out of the oven and put in the fridge for at least 4 hours or overnight.
13. Serve cold.

TURRONES DE MANÍ (PEANUT BRITTLE):

INGREDIENTS:

- 1 cup granulated sugar
- 1/2 cup light corn syrup
- 1 cup roasted peanuts
- 1 tsp baking soda
- 1 tsp vanilla extract

- Pinch of salt

Instructions:

1. Put parchment paper on a baking sheet and set it aside.
2. Over medium-high heat, stir the powdered sugar and corn syrup in a saucepan until the sugar melts.
3. Keep cooking without moving until a candy thermometer reads 300°F (150°C) or the mixture turns a deep amber color.
4. Add the baking soda, vanilla extract, and a pinch of salt quickly after taking the pan off the heat.
5. Spread the dough out with a spoon after pouring it onto the baking sheet that has been prepared.
6. After it has cooled down and become hard, break it up.
7. Put in a jar that won't let air in.

CREMA DE VIE:

INGREDIENTS:

- 4 large eggs
- 1 (14 oz) can sweetened condensed milk
- 1 (12 oz) can evaporated milk
- 1/2 cup rum (or more to taste)
- 1 tsp vanilla extract
- Ground cinnamon for garnish (optional)

Instructions:

1. Put the eggs, sweetened condensed milk, evaporated milk, rum, and vanilla extract in a blender. Mix until it's smooth.
2. Put the mix into jars or bottles.
3. Please put it in the fridge for at least a few hours or overnight to let the flavors mix.
4. If you want, you can serve it cold and add it with ground cinnamon.

PLÁTANOS EN TENTACIÓN (CARAMELIZED PLANTAINS):

INGREDIENTS:

- 4 ripe plantains, peeled and sliced diagonally
- 1 cup brown sugar
- 1/2 cup water
- 1/4 cup unsalted butter
- 1 tsp ground cinnamon
- Pinch of salt

Instructions:

1. Brown sugar, water, butter, ground cinnamon, and a pinch of salt should all be put in a big skillet.
2. Stir the mixture over medium-low heat until the sugar melts and the mixture gets thicker.
3. Place the plantain slices in the pan and cook for 5 to 7 minutes on each side until they get soft and browned.

4. The Plátanos en Tentación should be served hot.

CUBAN CHOCOLATE POTS DE CRÈME:

INGREDIENTS:

- 1 cup heavy cream
- 1 cup whole milk
- 4 oz semisweet chocolate, chopped
- 1/4 cup granulated sugar
- 4 large egg yolks
- 1 tsp vanilla extract
- Pinch of salt
- Whipped cream and chocolate shavings for garnish (optional)

Instructions:

1. Warm the oven up to 160°C (325°F). In a large baking dish, put six ramekins.
2. Add the whole milk and heavy cream to a pot. Place the saucepan over medium-low heat. Take it off the heat.
3. Mix the chocolate chips into the hot cream and let them melt for a few minutes. Mix until it's smooth.
4. Mix the granulated sugar, egg whites, vanilla extract, and a pinch of salt in a different bowl using a whisk.
5. Pour the chocolate mixture into the egg mixture slowly while mixing all the time to mix.
6. After straining the mixture through a fine-mesh sieve, put it into a pitcher or bowl.

7. Put the ramekins in the baking dish and pour the filling into them.
8. Boil enough water to come halfway up the sides of the ramekins in the baking dish.
9. Place the baking dish in a warm oven and cover it with aluminum foil. Bake for 30 to 35 minutes, or until the pots de crème are set around the edges but still wobbly in the middle.
10. Remove them from the oven and put them in the water bath to cool down. After that, put it in the fridge for at least four hours or overnight.
11. If you want, you can serve it cold with whipped cream and chocolate shavings on top.

MERENGUITOS (MERINGUE COOKIES):

INGREDIENTS:

- 3 large egg whites
- 1 cup granulated sugar
- 1 tsp vanilla extract
- Pinch of salt
- Food coloring (optional)

Instructions:

1. Warm the oven up to 225°F (110°C). Put parchment paper on the bottom of a baking sheet.

2. With a pinch of salt, beat the egg whites in a clean, dry bowl until they foam up.
3. Add the powdered sugar slowly, one tablespoon, while simultaneously beating the egg whites. Beat until peaks form that are stiff and shiny.
4. If you are using food coloring, add it now, along with the vanilla extract.
5. Place spoonfuls of meringue on the baking sheet that has been made.
6. Before you put the cookies in the oven, heat it. Bake them for about 1.5 to 2 hours or until dry and crisp.
7. Turn off the oven and let the cookies cool down inside.
8. After the Merenguitos have cooled, please put them in a container that won't let air in.

CINNAMON SUGAR CHURRO BITES:

INGREDIENTS:

- 1 cup water
- 2 1/2 tbsp granulated sugar
- 1/2 tsp salt
- 2 tbsp vegetable oil
- 1 cup all-purpose flour
- 2 quarts vegetable oil for frying
- 1/2 cup granulated sugar (for coating)
- 1 tsp ground cinnamon (for coating)

Instructions:

1. Fill a pot with water. Add salt, 2 1/2 tablespoons of sugar, and 2 tablespoons of vegetable oil. Bring up the temperature.
2. Take it off the heat and add the flour. Mix it in until it makes a dough ball.
3. Heat the 2 quarts of vegetable oil to 375°F (190°C) in a deep fryer or big pot.
4. Put the dough in a pastry bag that has a star-shaped tip.
5. Slice the dough into little squares and drop them into the hot oil.
6. Do not take the churro bites out of the oil until golden brown. Use a forked spoon to take them out and let them drain on paper towels.
7. Mix the rest of the sugar and ground cinnamon in a small dish.
8. To cover the warm churro bites, roll them in the cinnamon-sugar mix.
9. Serve right away.

GUAVA AND CHEESE EMPANADAS:

INGREDIENTS:

- 1 package of frozen empanada dough rounds, thawed
- 1 cup guava paste, cut into small cubes
- 1 cup cream cheese
- 1 egg, beaten (for egg wash)

Instructions:

1. Warm your oven to the temperature listed on the empanada dough package, usually around 190°C or 375°F.
2. Put a small amount of guava paste and cream cheese in the middle of each round of empanada dough.
3. Cut the dough in half and fold it to make a half-moon form. Seal the edges with a fork.
4. The egg wash will give the empanadas a golden color.
5. The empanadas should be put on a baking sheet with parchment paper.
6. Once the oven is hot, put the empanadas in it for 15 to 20 minutes or until golden brown.
7. Let them cool down a bit before you serve them.

CUBAN RICE PUDDING FLAN (FLAN DE ARROZ CON LECHE):

INGREDIENTS: For the Rice Pudding Layer:

- 1 cup long-grain white rice
- 2 cups water
- 1 cinnamon stick
- 1/4 tsp salt
- 4 cups whole milk
- 1 cup granulated sugar
- 1 tsp vanilla extract For the Flan Layer:
- 1 cup granulated sugar
- 1/4 cup water

- 4 large eggs
- 1 can (14 oz) sweetened condensed milk
- 1 can (12 oz) evaporated milk
- 1 tsp vanilla extract

Instructions: For the Rice Pudding Layer:

1. Run cold water over the rice until the water runs clear, then drain.
2. Put the rice, 2 cups of water, cinnamon stick, and salt in a pot. Bring up the temperature.
3. Turn down the heat, cover, and let it simmer for about 15 minutes, or until the rice is soft and the water is gone.
4. Put the milk, sugar, and vanilla extract in a different pot. Heat them over medium-low heat until the sugar melts.
5. After adding the cooked rice to the milk mixture, stir it and cook for another 20 to 25 minutes, or until the mixture gets thicker and the rice pudding is smooth.
6. Take the cinnamon stick off the heat and throw it away.
7. Fill a flan pan or baking dish with caramel and pour the rice pudding into it. Put away.
8. For the flan layer: 8. Put 1/4 cup of water and 1 cup of granulated sugar in a different pot. Stir the mixture on medium heat until the sugar is gone.
9. Don't stir the liquid again until it turns into caramel and is a golden brown color.
10. Be careful as you pour the hot caramel on top of the layer of rice pudding in the flan shape or baking dish.
11. Put the eggs, sweetened condensed milk, evaporated milk, and vanilla extract in a blender. Mix until it's smooth.
12. Put the flan mix in the dish or shape on the caramel layer.
13. Stick a tight piece of aluminum foil over the shape or dish.

14. Put the mold or dish in a bigger pan full of hot water. This will make a water bath.
15. Preheat the oven to 350°F (175°C). Bake the flan for about 1.5 to 2 hours, or until it's set but still has a little give in the middle.
16. Take it out of the oven and let it cool down until it's even.
17. Please put it in the fridge for at least four hours or overnight.
18. To serve, run a knife around the flan's edge, flip it onto a plate, and drizzle the caramel over the layer of rice pudding.

CUBAN GUAVA BARS:

INGREDIENTS: For the Crust:

- 1 1/2 cups all-purpose flour
- 1/2 cup granulated sugar
- 1/4 tsp salt
- 3/4 cup unsalted butter, cold and cubed. For the Guava Filling:
- 1 cup guava paste, cut into small cubes
- 2 tbsp all-purpose flour
- 1 tbsp water
- Powdered sugar for dusting (optional)

Instructions: For the Crust:

1. Warm the oven up to 175°F (350°F). Line a 9x9-inch baking dish with parchment paper, leaving two sides of the paper hanging over the edges. Grease the paper.
2. Blend the flour, sugar, and salt in a food processor. Press and hold to mix.
3. Put the cold, cubed butter into the food processor and pulse it a few times to make a mixture that looks like small crumbs.
4. Spread the mix evenly in the baking dish that has been prepared.
5. After the hot oven, bake for 20 to 25 minutes or until the crust is barely crispy.
6. For the filling made of guava: 6. The guava paste, 2 tablespoons of flour, and 1 tablespoon of water should all be mixed in a pot.
7. Keep stirring the guava paste while cooking on low heat until it gets smooth and bubbles.
8. Mix the guava filling well with the baked shell after you pour it on top.
9. Put the baking dish back in the oven and bake for 15 to 20 minutes or until the filling is set.
10. Please remove it from the oven and leave it in the dish to cool down.
11. When the guava bars are fully relaxed, use the extra parchment paper to lift them out of the dish.
12. If you want, you can dust them with powdered sugar and cut them into pieces or bars.

TORREJAS (CUBAN-STYLE FRENCH TOAST):

INGREDIENTS:

- 4 thick slices of Cuban or French bread
- 2 cups whole milk
- 3 large eggs
- 1/4 cup granulated sugar
- 1 tsp ground cinnamon
- 1/2 tsp vanilla extract
- Butter or oil for frying
- Maple syrup or honey for serving
- Fresh fruit for garnish (optional)

Instructions:

1. Mix the milk, eggs, sugar, ground cinnamon, and vanilla extract for a small dish with a whisk.
2. Put a pan or griddle over medium-high heat and add oil or butter.
3. Spread out the bread slices and dip each one into the milk mixture. Let each side soak for a short time.
4. When the pan is hot, add the wet bread slices. Cook for about two to three minutes on each side until both sides are golden brown.
5. Take it out of the pan and let it drain on paper towels.
6. If you want, you can top the warm Torrejas with fresh fruit and maple syrup or honey.

ARROZ CON MAÍZ (CUBAN SWEET CORN RICE):

INGREDIENTS:

- 1 cup long-grain white rice
- 2 cups water
- 1 cup sweet corn kernels (fresh or frozen)
- 1/4 cup unsalted butter
- 1/4 cup granulated sugar
- 1/4 tsp salt
- 1/4 cup whole milk
- 1/4 tsp ground cinnamon
- 1/4 tsp vanilla extract
- Fresh cilantro leaves for garnish (optional)

Instructions:

1. Run cold water over the rice until the water runs clear, then drain.
2. Put the rice, 2 cups of water, and sweet corn kernels in a pot. Bring up the temperature.
3. Turn down the heat, cover, and let it simmer for about 15 minutes, or until the rice is soft and the water is gone.
4. Melt the butter over low heat in a different pot. The salt, whole milk, ground cinnamon, and vanilla extract should all be mixed. Stir the food while it's cooking until all the sugar is gone.
5. Pour the milk mix over the corn and rice that have been cooked. Use a stir to mix.
6. Cover the Arroz con Maíz and let it cook on deficient heat for another 10 to 15 minutes. This will give the tastes time to blend.
7. If you want, you can serve it warm with fresh cilantro leaves on top.

COCONUT FLAN:

INGREDIENTS: For the Flan Layer:

- 1 cup granulated sugar
- 1/4 cup water
- 4 large eggs
- 1 can (14 oz) sweetened condensed milk
- 1 can (12 oz) evaporated milk
- 1 can (13.5 oz) coconut milk
- 1 tsp vanilla extract For the Coconut Layer:
- 1 cup shredded coconut

Instructions: For the Flan Layer:

1. Put 1/4 cup of water and 1 cup of granulated sugar in a pot. Stir the mixture on medium heat until the sugar is gone.
2. Don't stir the liquid again until it turns into caramel and is a golden brown color.
3. Be careful when pouring hot caramel into a flan shape or baking dish. Swirl the pan to cover the bottom evenly.
4. For the layer of coconut: 4. Spread the coconut flakes out evenly on top of the caramel layer.
5. To make the flan mix: 5. Sweetened condensed milk, evaporated milk, coconut milk, and vanilla extract should all be put into a mixer. Mix until it's smooth.
6. Put the flan mix in the dish or shape on the coconut layer.

7. How to Bake: 7. Stick a tight aluminum foil over the shape or dish.
8. Put the mold or dish in a bigger pan full of hot water. This will make a water bath.
9. Preheat the oven to 350°F (175°C). Bake the flan for about 1.5 to 2 hours, or until it's set but still has a little give in the middle.
10. Take it out of the oven and let it cool down until it's even.
11. Please put it in the fridge for at least four hours or overnight.
12. To serve, run a knife around the flan's edge, flip it onto a plate, and drizzle the caramel over the coconut layer.

MANGO SORBET:

INGREDIENTS:

- 4 ripe mangoes, peeled, pitted, and chopped
- 1/2 cup granulated sugar
- 1/4 cup water
- 2 tbsp fresh lime juice

Instructions:

1. Put the water and powdered sugar in a saucepan and mix them. Stir the sugar into the water over medium heat until it melts. This will make a simple syrup.
2. Wait until the simple syrup is cool enough to touch.
3. Put the chopped mangoes, simple syrup, and fresh lime juice in a blender.
4. Mix until it's smooth.

5. Put the mango mixture into an ice cream maker and churn it as directed by the maker's maker.
6. Put the mango sorbet in a jar that won't let air in. Freeze for a few hours or until it's firm.
7. Serve cold.

PASTEL DE MALANGA (MALANGA CAKE):

INGREDIENTS:

- 2 lbs malanga root, peeled and grated
- 1 cup granulated sugar
- 1/2 cup unsalted butter, melted
- 1 cup whole milk
- 3 large eggs
- 1 tsp vanilla extract
- 1/4 tsp salt
- 1/4 tsp ground cinnamon
- Powdered sugar for dusting (optional)

Instructions:

1. Warm the oven up to 175°F (350°F). Prepare a 9x13-inch baking dish by greasing it.
2. Grate the malanga and mix it with the sugar, melted butter, whole milk, eggs, vanilla extract, salt, and ground cinnamon in a big bowl. Combine well.
3. Put the mix into the baking dish that has been prepared.

4. Heat the oven to 350°F. Bake the cake for 45 to 50 minutes until the top is golden brown and the center is set.
5. Before cutting the Pastel de Malanga, let it cool down.
6. Add powdered sugar on top if you like.

MANTECADOS (CUBAN SHORTBREAD COOKIES):

INGREDIENTS:

- 1 cup unsalted butter, softened
- 1/2 cup granulated sugar
- 1 tsp vanilla extract
- 2 cups all-purpose flour
- 1/4 cup cornstarch
- Powdered sugar for dusting

Instructions:

1. Warm the oven up to 175°F (350°F). Put parchment paper on the bottom of a baking sheet.
2. Cream the softened butter, sugar, and vanilla extract together until the mixture is light and fluffy.
3. Add the cornstarch and all-purpose flour and mix them in until the dough comes together.
4. Use cookie tools to make rounds out of the dough or roll it into small balls.
5. Once the baking sheet is ready, put the cookies on it.

6. After the oven is hot, bake the cookies for 15 to 18 minutes or until they are set but not browned.
7. Place the Mantecados on a wire rack to cool down.
8. Before you serve, sprinkle with powdered sugar.

GUAVA PASTRIES (PASTELITOS DE GUAYABA):

INGREDIENTS:

- 1 package of frozen puff pastry sheets, thawed
- 1 cup guava paste, cut into small cubes
- 1/4 cup cream cheese
- 1 egg, beaten (for egg wash)
- Powdered sugar for dusting (optional)

Instructions:

1. Warm your oven to the temperature listed on the puff pastry package, usually around 190°C or 375°F.
2. To make a 1/4-inch thick sheet, roll out the cold puff pastry on a lightly floured surface.
3. You can cut the dough into quarters or rectangles, whichever you like better.
4. In the middle of each piece of pastry, put a small cube of guava paste and a teaspoon of cream cheese.
5. Use a fork to seal the sides of the pastry as you fold it over to make a triangle or rectangle.
6. For a golden look, brush the cakes with egg wash.

7. Pastries should be put on a baking sheet lined with parchment paper.
8. Heat the oven and put the cakes in it. Bake for 15 to 20 minutes or until golden brown and puffy.
9. Let them cool down a bit before you serve them. If you want, you can sprinkle them with powdered sugar.

MANGO TRES LECHES CAKE:

INGREDIENTS: For the Cake:

- 1 1/2 cups all-purpose flour
- 1 1/2 tsp baking powder
- 1/2 tsp salt
- 4 large eggs
- 1 cup granulated sugar
- 1 tsp vanilla extract
- 1/2 cup whole milk
- 1/2 cup mango puree For the Tres Leches Sauce:
- 1 can (14 oz) sweetened condensed milk
- 1 can (12 oz) evaporated milk
- 1 cup heavy cream
- 1/2 cup mango puree For the Topping:
- 2 cups whipped cream
- Fresh mango slices for garnish (optional)

Instructions: For the Cake:

1. Warm the oven up to 175°F (350°F). A 9x13-inch baking dish should be greased and floured.
2. There is all-purpose flour, baking powder, and salt in a bowl. Mix them with a whisk.
3. Beat the eggs and sugar in a different bowl until the mixture is light and foamy.
4. Add the vanilla extract and mix well.
5. Slowly add the dry ingredients to the egg mixture while occasionally mixing milk and mango puree. Put the dry ingredients in first and end with them.
6. When the baking dish is ready, pour the batter and spread it evenly.
7. After the oven is hot, bake it for 25 to 30 minutes or until a toothpick stuck in the middle comes out clean.
8. Take the cake out of the oven and let it cool down.
9. How to make the Tres Leches Sauce: 9. Put the evaporated milk, heavy cream, sweetened condensed milk, and mango puree in a blender. Mix until it's smooth.
10. Use a fork to poke holes in the cake while it's still warm.
11. Cover the warm cake with the Tres Leches sauce and let it soak in. Please put it in the fridge for at least two hours or overnight.
12. As for the topping: 12. Cover the cold cake with whipped cream.
13. If you want, you can add fresh mango pieces as a garnish.
14. Serve cold.

GUANÁBANA ICE CREAM:

INGREDIENTS:

- 2 cups guanábana (soursop) pulp, fresh or frozen
- 1 cup granulated sugar
- 2 cups heavy cream
- 1 tsp vanilla extract

Instructions:

1. Use a mixer to mix the granulated sugar and guanábana pulp. Mix until it's smooth.
2. Put the vanilla extract and heavy cream into the blender. Blend until everything is well mixed.
3. Put the liquid into an ice cream maker and churn it as directed by the maker's maker.
4. Put the guanábana ice cream in a container that won't let air in. Freeze for a few hours or until it's hard.
5. Serve cold.

CAFÉ CUBANO AFFOGATO:

INGREDIENTS:

- 1 shot of strong Cuban coffee
- 1 scoop of vanilla ice cream
- Chocolate shavings or cocoa powder for garnish (optional)

Instructions:

1. Make a solid Cuban coffee drink.

2. Put a scoop of vanilla ice cream in a bowl or glass to serve.
3. Put the hot coffee on top of the ice cream.
4. Add chocolate bits or cocoa powder as a garnish if you like.
5. Serve your Café Cubano Affogato right away and enjoy it!

PINEAPPLE EMPANADAS:

INGREDIENTS:

- 1 package of frozen empanada dough rounds, thawed
- 2 cups fresh pineapple, finely chopped
- 1/2 cup granulated sugar
- 1/2 tsp ground cinnamon
- 1 egg, beaten (for egg wash)

Instructions:

1. Warm your oven to the temperature listed on the empanada dough package, usually around 190°C or 375°F.
2. Chop the pineapple and put it in a bowl. Add the sugar and ground cinnamon. Combine well.
3. Put some of the pineapple filling inmiddle of each round of empanada dough.
4. Cut the dough in half and fold it to make a half-moon form. Seal the edges with a fork.
5. The egg wash will giwith parchment paperr.

6. The empanadas should be put on a baking sheet with parchment paper on i
7. e oven is hot, put the empanadas in it for 15 to 20 minutes or until they turn golden brown.
8. Let them cool down a bit before you serve them.

GUAVA MOUSSE:

INGREDIENTS:

- 1 cup guava puree
- 1/2 cup granulated sugar
- 2 cups heavy cream
- 1 tsp vanilla extract
- Fresh guava slices for garnish (option

uctions:

1. Put the powdered sugar and guava puree in a bowl and mix them. Mix the sugar in until it's gone.
2. Mix the heavy cream and vanilla extract in a different bowl and beat them together until stiff peaks form.
3. Mix the guava mixture into the whipped cream slowly until everything is well-mixed.
4. Put the guava mousse into bowls or glasses to serve.
5. If you want, you can add fresh guava pieces as a garnish.
6. Please put it in the fridge for a few hours before you serve it.
7. Serve cold.

QUESILLO (CUBAN FLAN):

INGREDIENTS: For the Caramel:

- 1 cup granulated sugar
- 1/4 cup water For the Flan:
- 4 large eggs
- 1 can (14 oz) sweetened condensed milk
- 1 can (12 oz) evaporated milk
- 1 tsp vanilla extract

*Instruction*e Caramel:

1. Put the owdered sugar in a saucepan and mix them. Stir the mixture on medium heat until the sugar is gone.
2. Don't stir the liquid pouringit turns into caramel and is a golden brown color.
3. Be careful when pouring hot caramel into a flan shape or baking dish. Swirl the pan to cover the bottom evenly.
4. To make the flan: 4. Put the eggs, sweetened condensed milk, evaporated min the dish or shape ilk, and vanilla extract in it's smooth.
5. Put the flan mix on top of the caramel layer in tPut the mold or dish in dish or shape.
6. Stick a tight pover the shape or dish.
7. Put the mold or dish in a bigger pan full of hot water. This will make a water bath.

8. Preheat the oven to 350°F (175°C). Bake the flan for about 1.5 to 2 hours, or until it's set but still has a little give in the middle.
9. Take it out of the oven and let it cool down until it's even.
10. Please put it in the fridge for at least hours or overnight.
11. To serve, run a knife around the flan's edge, flip it onto a plate, and drizzle the caramel.

PLÁTANOS MADUROS FRITOS (FRIED SWEET PLANTAINS):

INGREDIENTS:

- Ripe plantains, peeled and sliced diagonally
- Vegetable oil for frying
- Salt to taste

Instructions:

1. Put vegetable oil in a pan and heat it over medium-high heat.
2. Toast the plantain slices in a pan until both sides are golden brown.
3. Take it out of the pan and let it drain on paper towels.
4. Add salt to your liking.
5. You can eat the Plátanos Maduros Fritos as a snack or side dish.

CHOCOLATE TURRÓN:

INGREDIENTS:

- 2 cups semisweet chocolate chips
- 1 cup creamy peanut butter
- 1/2 cup granulated sugar
- 1/4 cup unsalted butter
- 1 tsp vanilla extract
- 2 cups crispy rice cereal
- 1 cup roasted peanuts

Instructions:

1. Cover a 9x9-inch baking dish with parchment paper, leaving two sides that hangover.
2. Mix the semisweet chocolate chips, creamy peanut butter, powdered sugar, and unsalted butter in a bowl that cae microwave.
3. To smooth the mixture, microwave it for 30 seconds and stir it after each.
4. It's time to add the vanilla extract.
5. As you mix the crispy rice cereal and roasted peanuts, ensure they are covered evenly in chocolate.
6. Press the mix into the baking dish that has been prepared.
7. The Chocolate Turrón should be put in the fridge for a few hours or until it sets.
8. Use the extra pieces of parchment paper to lift the turrón out of the dish and cut it into squares or bars.

GUAVA AND CREAM CHEESE TART:

INGREDIENTS: For the Tart Crust:

- 1 1/4 cups all-purpose flour
- 1/4 cup granulated sugar
- 1/2 tsp salt
- 1/2 cup unsalted butter, cold and cubed
- 1 large egg yolk
- 2 tbsp ice water For the Filling:
- 8 oz cream cheese, softened
- 1/4 cup granulated sugar
- 1 large egg
- 1 tsp vanilla extract
- 1/2 cup guava paste, cut into small cubes

Instructions: For the Tart Crust:

1. Blend the all-purpose flour, granulated sugar, and salt in a food processor. Press and hold to mix.
2. Put the cold, cubed butter into the food processor and pulse it a few times to make a mixture that looks like small crumbs.
3. Mix the egg yolk and ice water in a small bowl.
4. Adding the egg yolk mixture to the dough while the food processor is going will help it come together.
5. Put the dough in the fridge for at least 30 minutes after making a ball out of it.
6. Warm the oven up to 190°C (375°F). Roll out the cold dough on a floured surface and fit it into a tart pan.
7. Use a fork to poke holes in the bottom of the crust.

8. After the hot oven, bake for about 15 minutes or until the crust is barely crispy.
9. To make the filling: 9. Put the softened cream cheese in a bowl and beat it until it's smooth.
10. Put the egg, vanilla extract, and powdered sugar in the bowl. Mix everything by beating it.
11. If the tart crust is only partly cooked, pour the cream cheese filling into it.
12. Put the cubes of guava paste on top of the filling.
13. After taking the tart out of the oven, bake it for another 20 to 25 minutes or until the filling is set and golden.
14. Wait until the tart is excellent to cut and serve.

CUBAN COFFEE PANNA COTTA:

INGREDIENTS:

- 1 cup heavy cream
- 1 cup whole milk
- 1/2 cup strong Cuban coffee, cooled
- 1/2 cup granulated sugar
- 2 tsp unflavored gelatin
- 2 tbsp cold water
- 1 tsp vanilla extract

Instructions:

1. Put cold water in a small bowl and sprinkle the gelatin over it. Let it grow for five minutes.

2. Mix the powdered sugar, heavy cream, whole milk, and Cuban coffee in a saucepan. Stir the mixture over medium-low heat until the sugar is gone and hot but not boiling.
3. After removing the pan from the heat, add the vanilla extract and stir it.
4. Mix the blooming gelatin into the hot mixture and mix it in with a whisk until it's all gone.
5. Put the mix into ramekins or glasses for serving.
6. Please put in the fridge for at least four hours or until it sets.
7. Serve cold.

ARROZ CON DULCE (CUBAN RICE PUDDING):

INGREDIENTS:

- 1 cup long-grain white rice
- 2 cups water
- 1 cinnamon stick
- 1/4 tsp salt
- 4 cups whole milk
- 1 cup granulated sugar
- 1 tsp vanilla extract
- 1/2 cup raisins (optional)
- Ground cinnamon for garnish

Instructions:

1. Run cold water over the rice until the water runs clear, then drain.
2. Put the rice, 2 cups of water, cinnamon stick, and salt in a pot. Bring up the temperature.
3. Turn down the heat, cover, and let it simmer for about 15 minutes, or until the rice is soft and the water is gone.
4. Put the milk, granulated sugar, and vanilla extract in a different pot. Heat them over medium-low heat until the sugar melts.
5. After adding the cooked rice to the milk mixture, stir it and cook for another 20 to 25 minutes, or until the mixture gets thicker and the rice pudding is smooth.
6. Add the raisins to the rice pudding after you've cooked it.
7. Take the cinnamon stick off the heat and throw it away.
8. Arroz con Dulce should be served in bowls or dishes.
9. To finish, sprinkle with ground cinnamon.
10. Serve hot or cold.

COCONUT RICE PUDDING:

INGREDIENTS:

- 1 cup long-grain white rice
- 2 cups water
- 1 can (13.5 oz) coconut milk
- 1 can (14 oz) sweetened condensed milk
- 1 tsp vanilla extract
- 1/4 tsp salt
- Ground cinnamon for garnish (optional)

Instructions:

1. Run cold water over the rice until the water runs clear, then drain.
2. Put the rice, 2 cups of water, and a pinch of salt in a pot. Bring up the temperature.
3. Turn down the heat, cover, and let it simmer for about 15 minutes, or until the rice is soft and the water is gone.
4. Over medium heat, mix the sweetened condensed milk, vanilla extract, and 1/4 tsp salt in a different saucepan until the mixture is hot and well-mixed.
5. Add the cooked rice to the coconut milk mixture. Cook, turning often, for another 10 to 15 minutes or until the mixture thickens and the rice pudding is smooth.
6. Take it off the heat.
7. Put the Coconut Rice Pudding into bowls or plates that will be used for serving.
8. If you want, you can decorate with ground cinnamon.
9. Serve hot or cold.

GUAVA AND CREAM CHEESE PASTRIES:

INGREDIENTS:

- 1 package of frozen puff pastry sheets, thawed
- 1/2 cup guava paste, cut into small cubes
- 1/2 cup cream cheese
- 1 egg, beaten (for egg wash)

- Powdered sugar for dusting (optional)

Instructions:

1. Warm your oven to the temperature listed on the puff pastry package, usually around 200°C or 400°F.
2. First, let the puff pastry sheets thaw. Then, roll them out on a lightly floured surface.
3. You can cut the pastry sheets into squares or quarters, whichever you prefer.
4. Use a spoon to put guava paste and cream cheese in the middle of each dough square.
5. Fold the dough in half to make a triangle or rectangle, then press the sides with a fork to seal them.
6. For a golden look, brush the cakes with egg wash.
7. Pastries should be put on a baking sheet lined with parchment paper.
8. After the oven is hot, bake the cakes for 15 to 20 minutes or until golden and puffy.
9. Let them cool down a bit before you serve them.
10. Add powdered sugar on top if you like.

GUAVA AND CHEESE FLAN:

INGREDIENTS: For the Caramel:

- 1 cup granulated sugar
- 1/4 cup water For the Flan:
- 4 large eggs
- 1 can (14 oz) sweetened condensed milk

- 1 can (12 oz) evaporated milk
- 1 cup cream cheese
- 1 cup guava paste, cut into small cubes
- 1 tsp vanilla extract

Instructions: For the Caramel:

1. Put the water and powdered sugar in a saucepan and mix them. Stir the mixture on medium heat until the sugar is gone.
2. Don't stir the liquid again until it turns into caramel and is a golden brown color.
3. Be careful when pouring hot caramel into a flan shape or baking dish. Swirl the pan to cover the bottom evenly.
4. To make the flan: 4. The eggs, evaporated milk, sweetened condensed milk, cream cheese, guava paste, and vanilla extract should all be put into a mixer. Mix until it's smooth.
5. Put the flan mix in the dish or shape on top of the caramel layer.
6. Stick a tight piece of aluminum foil over the shape or dish.
7. Put the mold or dish in a bigger pan full of hot water. This will make a water bath.
8. Preheat the oven to 350°F (175°C). Bake the flan for about 1.5 to 2 hours, or until it's set but still has a little give in the middle.
9. Take it out of the oven and let it cool down until it's even.
10. Please put it in the fridge for at least four hours or overnight.
11. To serve, run a knife around the flan's edge, flip it onto a plate, and drizzle the caramel over the layer of guava and cheese.

CARAMELIZED PINEAPPLE WITH RUM SAUCE:

INGREDIENTS:

- 1 pineapple, peeled, cored, and sliced into rings
- 1/2 cup granulated sugar
- 1/4 cup unsalted butter
- 1/4 cup dark rum
- Vanilla ice cream for serving (optional)

Instructions:

1. Warm up the unsalted butter in a big pan over medium-low heat.
2. Put the powdered sugar in the pan and stir until it melts and turns into caramel.
3. Slowly add the pineapple rings to the caramel. Cook for a few minutes on each side until the rings are golden brown and cooked.
4. Take the pineapple rings out of the pan and set them aside.
5. Put the dark rum in the pan and cook for one or two minutes until the alcohol disappears and the sauce gets thicker.
6. Add the rum sauce to the pineapple rings that have been toasted.
7. If you want, you can serve the Caramelized Pineapple with Rum Sauce with vanilla ice cream.

CUBAN CHOCOLATE TRUFFLES:

INGREDIENTS:

- 8 oz semisweet chocolate, chopped
- 1/2 cup heavy cream
- 2 tbsp unsalted butter
- 1 tsp vanilla extract
- Cocoa powder, finely chopped nuts, or shredded coconut for coating

Instructions:

1. Put the chopped semisweet chocolate in a bowl that can handle the heat.
2. Over medium heat, bring the heavy cream and unsalted butter to a simmer in a pot.
3. Add the hot milk to the chocolate chips and then pour it on top.
4. Set it down for one minute and then stir until the chocolate is smooth and melted.
5. Add the vanilla extract and mix well.
6. After putting the bowl in the fridge for at least two hours, or until the mixture is firm enough to handle, cover it.
7. If you want to make truffles, roll small amounts of the dough into balls.
8. Roll them in chocolate powder, chopped nuts, or shredded coconut to cover the truffles.
9. Spread the truffles out on a baking sheet lined with parchment paper.

10. Put in the fridge until firm.
11. Break up the Cuban Chocolate Truffles and serve them cold.

CHOCOLATE COCONUT BARS:

INGREDIENTS:

- 1 cup unsalted butter
- 1 1/2 cups graham cracker crumbs
- 1 1/2 cups shredded coconut
- 1 1/2 cups semisweet chocolate chips
- 1 can (14 oz) sweetened condensed milk
- 1 cup chopped nuts (e.g., walnuts or pecans)

Instructions:

1. Warm the oven up to 175°F (350°F). Prepare a 9x13-inch baking dish by greasing it.
2. Melt the unsalted butter in a bowl that can go in the microwave.
3. Mix the graham cracker crumbs and coconut shreds in a different bowl.
4. Add the melted butter to the crumbs and mix them.
5. Spread the mix evenly in the baking dish that has been prepared.
6. Put the semisweet chocolate chips on top of the crust.
7. Cover the chocolate chips with the sweetened condensed milk.
8. Add the chopped nuts on top.

9. After the oven is hot, bake for 25 to 30 minutes or until the edges are golden brown.
10. Before cutting the Chocolate Coconut Bars into pieces or bars, let them cool in the dish.

GUAVA ICE CREAM:

INGREDIENTS:

- 2 cups guava puree
- 1 cup granulated sugar
- 2 cups heavy cream
- 1 tsp vanilla extract

Instructions:

1. Put the powdered sugar and guava puree in a bowl and mix them. Mix the sugar in until it's gone.
2. Put the heavy cream and vanilla extract in the bowl until everything is well mixed.
3. Put the liquid into an ice cream maker and churn it as directed by the maker's maker.
4. Put the guava ice cream in a jar that won't let air in. Freeze for a few hours or until it's firm.
5. Serve cold.

TORREJAS DE CALABAZA (PUMPKIN FRENCH TOAST):

INGREDIENTS:

- 4 thick slices of Cuban or French bread
- 2 cups whole milk
- 3 large eggs
- 1/4 cup granulated sugar
- 1 tsp ground cinnamon
- 1/2 tsp vanilla extract
- Butter or oil for frying
- Maple syrup or honey for serving
- Fresh fruit for garnish (optional)

Instructions:

1. Mix the milk, eggs, sugar, ground cinnamon, and vanilla extract for a small dish with a whisk.
2. Put a pan or griddle over medium-high heat and add oil or butter.
3. Spread out the bread slices and dip each one into the milk mixture. Let each side soak for a short time.
4. When the pan is hot, add the wet bread slices. Cook for about two to three minutes on each side until both sides are golden brown.
5. Take it out of the pan and let it drain on paper towels.
6. You can top the warm Torrejas de Calabaza with fresh fruit and maple syrup or honey.

MANGO COCONUT RICE PUDDING:

INGREDIENTS:

- 1 cup long-grain white rice
- 2 cups water
- 1 cup coconut milk
- 1 can (14 oz) sweetened condensed milk
- 2 cups fresh mango, diced
- 1 tsp vanilla extract
- Ground cinnamon for garnish (optional)

Instructions:

1. Run cold water over the rice until the water runs clear, then drain.
2. Put the rice, 2 cups of water, and coconut milk in a pot. Bring up the temperature.
3. Lower the heat, cover, and let it cook for about 15 minutes or until the rice is soft and the liquid is gone.
4. Mix well with the vanilla extract, diced mango, and sweetened condensed milk.
5. Stir the mixture often as you cook for another 10 to 15 minutes or until it gets thicker and the rice pudding is creamy.
6. Take it off the heat.
7. Put the Mango Coconut Rice Pudding into bowls to serve.
8. If you want, you can decorate with ground cinnamon.
9. Serve hot or cold.

CINNAMON SUGAR PLANTAIN CHIPS:

INGREDIENTS:

- Ripe plantains, peeled and thinly sliced
- Vegetable oil for frying
- Cinnamon sugar mixture (1/4 cup granulated sugar + 1 tsp ground cinnamon) for coating

Instructions:

1. Put vegetable oil in a large skillet or frying pan and heat it over medium-high heat.
2. Add the plantain slices one at a time and fry them until they are crisp and golden brown.
3. Take it out of the oil and let it drain on paper towels.
4. Mix the cinnamon and sugar and sprinkle it over the warm plantain chips to cover them.
5. Wait until they're cool to serve.

GUAVA CUSTARD:

INGREDIENTS:

- 1 cup guava puree
- 1/2 cup granulated sugar
- 2 cups heavy cream
- 1 tsp vanilla extract
- 6 large egg yolks
- Fresh guava slices for garnish (optional)

Instructions:

1. Put the powdered sugar and guava puree in a bowl and mix them. Mix the sugar in until it's gone.
2. Put the vanilla extract and heavy cream in a pot. Heat them over medium-low heat until they are hot but not boiling.
3. Whisk the egg whites in a different bowl.
4. Whisk the hot cream mixture into the egg whites little by little.
5. Put the mixture back in the pot. Cook it over low heat while stirring it until it gets thick enough to coat the back of a spoon (about 170°F or 77°C).
6. Then, take it off the heat and stir in the guava mix.
7. Use a fine-mesh sieve to pour the custard into a clean bowl.
8. Fill cups or glasses with ice and pour the custard into them.
9. Please put in the fridge for at least four hours or until it sets.
10. If you want, you can add fresh guava pieces as a garnish.
11. Serve cold.

GUAVA AND CHEESE TURNOVERS:

INGREDIENTS:

- 1 package of frozen puff pastry sheets, thawed
- 1/2 cup guava paste, cut into small cubes
- 1/2 cup cream cheese

- 1 egg, beaten (for egg wash)
- Powdered sugar for dusting (optional)

Instructions:

1. Warm your oven to the temperature listed on the puff pastry package, usually around 200°C or 400°F.
2. First, let the puff pastry sheets thaw. Then, roll them out on a lightly floured surface.
3. You can cut the dough into quarters or rectangles, whichever you like better.
4. Use a spoon to put guava paste and cream cheese in the middle of each dough square.
5. Fold the dough in half to make a triangle or rectangle, then press the sides with a fork to seal them.
6. Brush the turnovers with the egg wash to make them glossy.
7. Put the tarts on a baking sheet that has parchment paper on it.
8. Before putting the tarts in the oven, heat it. Bake them for 15 to 20 minutes or until golden and puffy.
9. Let them cool down a bit before you serve them.
10. Add powdered sugar on top if you like.

BANANA FRITTERS (BUÑUELOS DE PLÁTANO):

INGREDIENTS:

- Ripe bananas, mashed

- 1/2 cup all-purpose flour
- 1/4 cup granulated sugar
- 1/4 cup milk
- 1/2 tsp baking powder
- 1/4 tsp salt
- Vegetable oil for frying
- Powdered sugar for dusting (optional)

Instructions:

1. Mix the ripe bananas with the all-purpose flour, sugar, milk, baking powder, and salt in a bowl. Mix everything well.
2. Put vegetable oil in a large skillet or frying pan and heat it over medium-high heat.
3. Spoon banana batter into the hot oil in small amounts.
4. Fry the patties until both sides are a golden brown color.
5. Take it out of the oil and let it drain on paper towels.
6. Add powdered sugar on top if you like.
7. The banana fritters should be served hot.

COCONUT RUM BALLS:

INGREDIENTS:

- 2 cups vanilla wafer cookies, crushed
- 1 cup shredded coconut
- 1 cup chopped nuts (e.g., walnuts or pecans)
- 1 cup powdered sugar
- 2 tbsp unsweetened cocoa powder

- 1/2 cup dark rum
- 1/4 cup light corn syrup
- Additional powdered sugar or shredded coconut for coating

Instructions:

1. Crush the vanilla wafer cookies and mix them with the shredded coconut, chopped nuts, powdered sugar, and unsweetened cocoa powder in a bowl. Combine well.
2. Mix the dark rum and light corn syrup in a different bowl.
3. Add the rum mixture to the dry ingredients until everything is well mixed.
4. You can cover the balls in more powdered sugar or shredded coconut after you roll them in it.
5. Put the Coconut Rum Balls on a baking sheet lined with parchment paper.
6. Put in the fridge until firm.
7. Serve cold.

PAPAYA SORBET:

INGREDIENTS:

- 2 cups fresh papaya, diced
- 1/2 cup granulated sugar
- 1/4 cup water
- 2 tbsp fresh lime juice

Instructions:

1. Put the water and powdered sugar in a saucepan and mix them. Stir the sugar into the water over medium heat until it melts. This will make a simple syrup.
2. Wait until the simple syrup is cool enough to touch.
3. Dice the papaya and put it in a mixer with simple syrup and fresh lime juice.
4. Mix until it's smooth.
5. Put the papaya mixture into an ice cream maker and churn it as directed by the maker's maker.
6. Put the papaya sorbet in a jar that won't let air in. Freeze for a few hours or until it's firm.
7. Serve cold.

CUBAN CHOCOLATE FONDUE:

INGREDIENTS:

- 8 oz semisweet chocolate, chopped
- 1/2 cup heavy cream
- 1/4 cup dark rum
- Assorted dippers (e.g., strawberries, banana slices, marshmallows, pound cake cubes)

Instructions:

1. Put the heavy cream and semisweet chocolate in a bowl that can go in the microwave.
2. Stir the mixture every 30 seconds while heating it in the microwave until it is smooth, and the chocolate is melted.
3. Add the dark rum and mix it in.

4. Move the Cuban Chocolate Fondue to a bowl that can handle heat or a fondue pot.
5. Serve with different kinds of diapers.

GUAVA AND CREAM CHEESE CUPCAKES:

INGREDIENTS: For the Cupcakes:

- 1 1/2 cups all-purpose flour
- 1 1/2 tsp baking powder
- 1/4 tsp salt
- 1/2 cup unsalted butter, softened
- 1 cup granulated sugar
- 2 large eggs
- 1 tsp vanilla extract
- 1/2 cup milk
- 1/2 cup guava puree
- 4 oz cream cheese, softened For the Guava Cream Cheese Frosting:
- 4 oz cream cheese, softened
- 1/4 cup unsalted butter, softened
- 1/4 cup guava puree
- 2 cups powdered sugar
- Guava paste or guava slices for garnish (optional)

Instructions: For the Cupcakes:

1. Warm the oven up to 175°F (350°F). You can line a muffin tin with cupcake cups.
2. Whisk the all-purpose flour, baking powder, and salt in a bowl. Put away.
3. Put the melted unsalted butter and granulated sugar in a different bowl and mix them until they are light and fluffy.
4. Add the eggs and beat well after each one one at a time. Add the vanilla extract and mix well.
5. Slowly add the dry ingredients to the wet ones, mixing them with the milk occasionally. Start with the dry ingredients and end with the milk. Don't mix any further than that.
6. The guava mush should be carefully mixed in.
7. Two-thirds of the way to the top of each cupcake container should be full of batter.
8. Cream cheese should be melted. In a different bowl, beat it until it's smooth.
9. Fill the middle of each cupcake with cream cheese. Use a stick to swirl the cream cheese into the batter.
10. After the oven is hot, bake the cupcakes for 18 to 20 minutes or until a toothpick stuck in the middle comes out clean.
11. For a few minutes, let the cupcakes cool in the muffin tin. Then, move them to a wire rack to cool fully.
12. Steps to make the Guava Cream Cheese Frosting: 12. Softened cream cheese and plain butter should be mixed until smooth.
13. Mix the powdered sugar and guava puree slowly until the frosting is smooth and creamy.
14. Use the Guava Cream Cheese Frosting to decorate the cupcakes once they are completely cool.
15. If you want, you can add guava paste or pieces of guava as a garnish.

16. Your Guava and Cream Cheese Cupcakes are ready to be served.

TARO ROOT PUDDING (PUDIN DE MALANGA):

INGREDIENTS:

- 2 cups taro root (malanga), peeled and grated
- 1/2 cup coconut milk
- 1/2 cup granulated sugar
- 2 large eggs
- 1/4 tsp vanilla extract
- Ground cinnamon for garnish (optional)

Instructions:

1. Warm the oven up to 175°F (350°F). Prepare a baking dish by greasing it.
2. Grate the taro root and put it in a bowl. Add the coconut milk, sugar, eggs, and vanilla extract. Mix everything well.
3. Put the taro root mix into the baking dish that has been oiled.
4. After the hot oven, bake the dish for 45 to 50 minutes or until the pudding is set and the top is golden brown.
5. Take it out of the oven and let it cool down until it's even.
6. If you want, you can decorate with ground cinnamon.
7. Cut your Taro Root Pudding into pieces and serve it.

CARAMEL FLAN CAKE:

INGREDIENTS: For the Caramel:

- 1 cup granulated sugar
- 1/4 cup water For the Flan:
- 4 large eggs
- 1 can (14 oz) sweetened condensed milk
- 1 can (12 oz) evaporated milk
- 1 tsp vanilla extract For the Cake:
- 1 1/2 cups all-purpose flour
- 1/2 cup granulated sugar
- 1/2 cup unsalted butter, softened
- 1/2 cup milk
- 1 tsp baking powder
- 1/4 tsp salt

Instructions: For the Caramel:

1. Put the water and powdered sugar in a saucepan and mix them. Stir the mixture while it's on medium heat until the sugar is gone.
2. Don't stir the liquid again until it turns into caramel and is a golden brown color.
3. Be careful when pouring hot caramel into a flan shape or baking dish. Swirl the pan to cover the bottom evenly.
4. To make the flan: 4. Put the eggs, sweetened condensed milk, evaporated milk, and vanilla extract in a blender. Mix until it's smooth.
5. Put the flan mix in the dish or shape on top of the caramel layer.

6. Stick a tight piece of aluminum foil over the shape or dish.
7. Put the mold or dish in a bigger pan full of hot water. This will make a water bath.
8. Preheat the oven to 350°F (175°C). Bake the flan for about 1.5 to 2 hours, or until it's set but still has a little give in the middle.
9. Take it out of the oven and let it cool down until it's even.
10. Please put it in the fridge for at least four hours or overnight.
11. To serve, run a knife around the flan's edge, flip it onto a plate, and drizzle the caramel.
12. Twelve for the cake. Warm the oven to 175°F (350°F)—butter and flour in a cake pan.
13. Mix the unsalted butter with the granulated sugar in a bowl until the mixture is light and fluffy.
14. Add the eggs and beat well after each one one at a time. Add the vanilla extract and mix well.
15. Mix the all-purpose flour, baking powder, and salt in a different bowl.
16. Slowly add the dry ingredients to the butter mixture, mixing them with the milk each time. Start with the dry ingredients and end with the milk. Don't mix any further than that.
17. Cover the flan layer in the cake pan with the cake batter.
18. After the oven is hot, bake the cake for 30 to 35 minutes or until a toothpick stuck in the middle comes out clean.
19. Put the cake on a serving plate after taking it out of the oven and letting it cool in the pan for a few minutes.
20. Cut your Caramel Flan Cake into pieces and serve it.

GUAVA AND CHEESE CROISSANTS:

INGREDIENTS:

- 1 package of crescent roll dough
- Guava paste, cut into small cubes
- Cream cheese
- Powdered sugar for dusting (optional)

Instructions:

1. Warm your oven to the temperature listed on the crescent roll dough package, usually around 190°C or 375°F.
2. Remove the crescent roll dough from the roll and cut it into pieces.
3. Put a cube of guava paste and a small amount of cream cheese at the wide end of each triangle.
4. Start rolling the squares up from the wide end to make crescent shapes.
5. Fill the crescents on a baking sheet lined with parchment paper.
6. Once the oven is hot, bake them for the time written on the dough package or until golden brown.
7. Let them cool down a bit before you serve them.
8. Add powdered sugar on top if you like.

GUAVA AND CHEESE PANCAKES:

INGREDIENTS:

- Pancake mix (prepared according to package instructions)
- Guava paste, cut into small cubes
- Cream cheese

Instructions:

1. Follow the directions on the package to make the pancake batter.
2. Put a griddle or nonstick pan over medium-low heat and lightly coat it with oil or butter.
3. Use the skillet to make pancakes by pouring pancake batter on it.
4. Put a few cubes of guava paste on each pancake and a few small spoonfuls of cream cheese.
5. As soon as the pancakes start to bubble on top and the edges look set, they are done.
6. After flipping, cook the other side until it's golden brown.
7. Your Guava and Cheese Pancakes are ready to be served after taking them off the flame.

COCONUT RICE CAKE:

INGREDIENTS:

- 2 cups glutinous rice
- 1 can (13.5 oz) coconut milk
- 1 cup granulated sugar

- 1/2 tsp salt
- 1 tsp vanilla extract
- 1/2 cup shredded coconut
- 1/2 cup coconut cream (for topping)

Instructions:

1. First, run cold water over the sticky rice until the water runs clear. Then, let the rice drain.
2. Mix the glutinous rice, coconut milk, sugar, and salt in a pot. Stir the mixture all the time over medium-low heat for about 20 to 25 minutes, or until it thickens and the rice is done.
3. Add the vanilla extract and mix well.
4. Take it off the heat and let it cool down a bit.
5. Cover the cooked rice in a baking dish that has been greased.
6. Put the coconut cream and chopped coconut in a different bowl. Add this to the rice and spread it out.
7. For a few minutes, or until the coconut topping is golden brown, broil the dish in the oven.
8. Before cutting and serving, let the Coconut Rice Cake cool down.

PINEAPPLE SORBET:

INGREDIENTS:

- 2 cups fresh pineapple chunks
- 1/2 cup granulated sugar

- 1/4 cup water
- 1 tbsp fresh lime juice

Instructions:

1. Put the water and powdered sugar in a saucepan and mix them. Stir the sugar into the water over medium heat until it melts. This will make a simple syrup.
2. Wait until the simple syrup is cool enough to touch.
3. Put the fresh pineapple chunks, simple syrup, and lime juice in a mixer.
4. Mix until it's smooth.
5. Put the pineapple mixture into an ice cream maker and churn it as directed by the maker's maker.
6. Put the pineapple sorbet in a jar that won't let air in. Freeze for a few hours or until it's firm.
7. Serve cold.

COCONUT RUM CAKE:

INGREDIENTS: For the Cake:

- 1 box (18.25 oz) yellow cake mix
- 1 package (3.4 oz) instant vanilla pudding mix
- 4 large eggs
- 1/2 cup vegetable oil
- 1/2 cup water
- 1/2 cup dark rum
- 1/2 cup shredded coconut For the Glaze:

- 1/2 cup unsalted butter
- 1/4 cup water
- 1 cup granulated sugar
- 1/2 cup dark rum

Instructions: For the Cake:

1. Warm the oven up to 160°C (325°F). Butter and flour in a bundt cake pan.
2. Put the eggs, vegetable oil, water, dark rum, shredded coconut, yellow cake mix, and instant vanilla pudding mix in a big bowl. Mix everything well.
3. When the bundt cake pan is ready, pour the cake batter into it.
4. After the oven is hot, bake the cake for 45 to 50 minutes or until a toothpick stuck in the middle comes out clean.
5. Take the cake out of the oven and let it cool for 10 minutes in the pan.
6. Flip the cake over onto a serving tray to let it cool down.
7. To make the glaze: 7. Put the unsalted butter, water, and powdered sugar in a saucepan. Stir the mixture on medium heat until the sugar is gone.
8. Take it off the heat and add the dark rum while stirring.
9. Use a fork or stick to make holes in the top of the cake while it is still warm.
10. Put the rum sauce on the hot cake and let it soak in.
11. Please wait until the Coconut Rum Cake is excellent and the glaze is set before you serve it.

MAMEY ICE CREAM:

INGREDIENTS:

- 2 cups mamey sapote flesh, peeled and seeded
- 1 cup granulated sugar
- 2 cups heavy cream
- 1 tsp vanilla extract

Instructions:

1. Mix the mamey sapote flesh and sugar into a smooth paste using a mixer. Mix until it's smooth.
2. Put the vanilla extract and heavy cream into the blender. Blend until everything is well mixed.
3. Put the liquid into an ice cream maker and churn it as directed by the maker's maker.
4. Put the mamey ice cream in a container that won't let air in. Freeze for a few hours or until it's hard.
5. Serve cold.

COCONUT CUSTARD PIE:

INGREDIENTS:

- 1 9-inch pie crust, prebaked
- 1 cup shredded coconut

- 1 cup granulated sugar
- 2 cups milk
- 4 large eggs
- 1 tsp vanilla extract
- 1/4 tsp salt
- Ground nutmeg for garnish (optional)

Instructions:

1. Warm the oven up to 175°F (350°F).
2. Cover the pie shell that has already been baked with the shredded coconut.
3. Put the milk in a pot and heat it over medium-low heat until it's hot but not boiling.
4. To make the frosting, put the granulated sugar, eggs, vanilla extract, and salt in a bowl and whisk them together.
5. Slowly add the hot milk to the egg mixture while whisking it in.
6. Spread the custard mix on top of the coconut shreds in the pie crust.
7. If you want, you can sprinkle ground nutmeg on top.
8. It should be baked in a hot oven for 40 to 45 minutes or until the custard is set and the top is barely browned.
9. Before cutting and serving, let the Coconut Custard Pie cool to room temperature.

PLANTAIN PUDDING (PUDÍN DE PLÁTANO):

INGREDIENTS:

- 4 ripe plantains, peeled and sliced
- 1 cup granulated sugar
- 2 cups milk
- 4 large eggs
- 1 tsp vanilla extract
- 1/4 tsp ground cinnamon
- 1/4 tsp salt
- Caramel sauce for drizzling (optional)

Instructions:

1. Warm the oven up to 175°F (350°F). Prepare a baking dish by greasing it.
2. Put the milk, powdered sugar, and sliced plantains in a saucepan. Stir the mixture occasionally while cooking over medium heat for about 15 to 20 minutes or until the plantains are soft and the sauce thickens.
3. Take it off the heat and let it cool down a bit.
4. Add the eggs, vanilla extract, ground cinnamon, and salt to a bowl and mix them using a whisk.
5. Mix the plantain mixture into the egg mixture slowly while whisking it in.
6. Place the plantain custard mix in the baking dish that has been coated.
7. Before you put it in the oven, heat it. Bake for 30 to 35 minutes until the top is golden brown and the pudding is set.
8. Before serving, let the Plantain Pudding cool down a bit.
9. If you want, drizzle with caramel sauce.

GUAVA AND CREAM CHEESE BROWNIES:

INGREDIENTS:

- 1 cup unsalted butter
- 2 cups granulated sugar
- 4 large eggs
- 1 tsp vanilla extract
- 1 cup all-purpose flour
- 1/2 cup unsweetened cocoa powder
- 1/4 tsp salt
- 1 cup cream cheese, softened
- 1/2 cup guava paste, softened and diced

Instructions:

1. Warm the oven up to 175°F (350°F). Prepare a 9x13-inch baking dish by greasing it.
2. Melt the unsalted butter over low heat in a pot.
3. After taking the pan off the heat, add the granulated sugar and stir until it is well mixed.
4. Adding the eggs one at a time and mixing them in is the next step.
5. All-purpose flour, unsweetened cocoa powder, and salt should all be mixed in a different bowl using a whisk.
6. Slowly add the dry ingredients to the butter mixture until everything is mixed.
7. Put the brownie batter into the baking dish that has been prepared.
8. The cream cheese and guava paste should be mixed in a different bowl until smooth.

9. Add dollops of the cream cheese mix to the cookie batter.
10. Swirl the cream cheese mixture into the brownie batter with a knife or stick to make it look like marble.
11. In a hot oven, bake for 30 to 35 minutes or until a toothpick stuck in the middle comes out with a few moist bits on it.
12. Before cutting the brownies into pieces, let them cool in the dish.

CUBAN COFFEE ICE CREAM:

INGREDIENTS:

- 2 cups heavy cream
- 1 cup whole milk
- 3/4 cup granulated sugar
- 1/2 cup Cuban coffee beans, coarsely ground
- 4 large egg yolks
- 2 tsp instant coffee granules (optional for extra coffee flavor)
- 1 tsp vanilla extract

Instructions:

1. Put the heavy cream, whole milk, sugar, and roughly ground Cuban coffee beans in a saucepan and mix them.
2. Over medium heat, stir the mixture now and then until it hits a slow simmer.
3. Cover the pan and take it off the heat. Let the coffee beans soak in the mixture for about 30 minutes.

4. Pour the mixture through a fine-mesh sieve into a different pot. Press down on the coffee beans to get the flavor out of them.
5. Whisk the egg whites together in a different bowl.
6. Slowly pour the coffee-infused mixture strained into the egg whites while whisking all the time.
7. Put the mixture back in the pot and stir it constantly over low heat until it gets thicker and coats the back of a spoon (about 170°F or 77°C).
8. Take the pan off the heat and add the vanilla extract and instant coffee grounds if you use them.
9. After letting the mixture cool to room temperature, put it in the fridge until it's cold.
10. After the liquid has been chilled, use an ice cream maker according to the directions that came with it.
11. Put the Cuban Coffee Ice Cream in a container that won't let air in. Freeze for a few hours or until it's hard.
12. Serve cold.

CINNAMON SUGAR CHURRO WAFFLES:

INGREDIENTS:

- 2 cups all-purpose flour
- 1/4 cup granulated sugar
- 1 tbsp baking powder
- 1 tsp ground cinnamon
- 1/4 tsp salt

- 2 large eggs
- 1 3/4 cups milk
- 1/3 cup unsalted butter, melted
- 1 tsp vanilla extract
- Cinnamon sugar mixture for coating (1/2 cup granulated sugar + 1 tsp ground cinnamon)
- Chocolate sauce, caramel sauce, or dulce de leche for drizzling (optional)

Instructions:

1. Follow the directions that came with your waffle pan to get it hot.
2. Mix the all-purpose flour, sugar, baking powder, ground cinnamon, and salt in a bowl using a whisk to make the dough.
3. Beat the eggs in a different bowl. Then, mix the milk, melted unsalted butter, and vanilla extract using a whisk.
4. Add the wet ingredients to the dry ones and mix them just until they are mixed.
5. Use nonstick food spray or a little melted butter to grease the waffle iron.
6. Pour the waffle batter onto a waffle iron that has already been cooked. Follow the directions on the waffle iron until the waffles are golden brown and crispy.
7. Add a lot of the cinnamon sugar mixture to the waffles while they are still warm to coat them.
8. You can drizzle it with chocolate sauce, caramel sauce, or dulce de leche.
9. Make sure to serve your Cinnamon Sugar Churro Waffles hot.

COCONUT MACAROONS:

INGREDIENTS:

- 3 cups shredded coconut
- 1/2 cup granulated sugar
- 1/4 cup all-purpose flour
- 1/4 tsp salt
- 4 large egg whites
- 1 tsp vanilla extract
- 1/2 tsp almond extract (optional)
- 4 oz semisweet chocolate, melted (for dipping, optional)

Instructions:

1. Warm the oven up to 160°C (325°F). Put parchment paper on the bottom of a baking sheet.
2. Put the powdered sugar, all-purpose flour, salt, and shredded coconut in a mixing bowl.
3. Whisk the egg whites in a different bowl until they make stiff peaks.
4. Add the egg whites that have been mixed slowly to the coconut mixture.
5. If you are using almond extract, mix it in with the vanilla extract.
6. Drop spoonfuls of the coconut mix onto the baking sheet that has been prepared and shape them into mounds.
7. Place the coconut macaroons in an oven that has already been warm. Bake for 20 to 25 minutes or until they are lightly golden.
8. They should cool down for a few minutes on the baking sheet before being moved to a wire rack.

9. You can dip the ends of the macaroons in melted semisweet chocolate if you want to. Then, put them on parchment paper to set.
10. Once the chocolate is hard, serve your Coconut Macaroons.

GUAVA SWIRL CHEESECAKE:

INGREDIENTS: For the Crust:

- 1 1/2 cups graham cracker crumbs
- 1/4 cup granulated sugar
- 1/2 cup unsalted butter, melted For the Cheesecake Filling:
- 24 oz cream cheese, softened
- 1 cup granulated sugar
- 4 large eggs
- 1 tsp vanilla extract
- 1/4 cup all-purpose flour
- 1/4 cup guava paste, softened and diced
- Guava sauce or puree for swirling (about 1/2 cup)

Instructions: For the Crust:

1. Warm the oven up to 160°C (325°F). Clean and grease a 9-inch springform pan.
2. Mix the graham cracker crumbs, sugar, and melted unsalted butter in a bowl. Mix until the bits are covered all over.

3. To make the crust, press the crumbs into the bottom of a springform pan that has been greased.
4. Please put it in an oven that is already hot for about 10 minutes. Take it out and put it somewhere to cool.
5. For the cheesecake filling: 5. Put the softened cream cheese in a big bowl and beat it until it is smooth and creamy.
6. Slowly add the granulated sugar and beat until everything is well mixed.
7. After adding the vanilla extract, beat the eggs one at a time.
8. Add the all-purpose flour and mix it in until it's just mixed.
9. On top of the shell that has cooled, pour the cheesecake filling.
10. In a bowl that can go in the microwave, heat the guava paste in short bursts while turning it until it's smooth.
11. Put small amounts of the guava paste that has been melted and the guava sauce or juice on top of the cheesecake filling.
12. Swirl the guava with a knife or stick to make the cheesecake look like marble.
13. After the oven is hot, bake the dish for 45 to 50 minutes or until the edges are set, and the middle is still wobbly.
14. Don't turn off the oven. Leave the cheesecake in there for another hour to cool down slowly.
15. Take the cheesecake out of the oven and put it in the fridge for at least 4 hours or overnight.

PINEAPPLE UPSIDE-DOWN CAKE:

INGREDIENTS: For the Topping:

- 1/4 cup unsalted butter
- 1 cup brown sugar
- 1 can (20 oz) pineapple slices in juice, drained (reserve juice)
- Maraschino cherries, for garnish For the Cake:
- 1 1/2 cups all-purpose flour
- 1 1/2 tsp baking powder
- 1/4 tsp salt
- 1/2 cup unsalted butter, softened
- 1 cup granulated sugar
- 2 large eggs
- 1 tsp vanilla extract
- 1/2 cup pineapple juice (reserved from the canned pineapple)
- 1/2 cup milk

Instructions: For the Topping:

1. Warm the oven up to 175°F (350°F). A 9x9-inch square baking pan should be greased.
2. Melt the unsalted butter over low heat in a pot.
3. Add the brown sugar and stir until it melts and the mixture looks like caramel.
4. Put the caramel mix in the baking pan that has been oiled.
5. Add the pineapple slices on top of the caramel. In the middle of each slice, put a maraschino cherry.
6. To Make the Cake: 6. Whisk the all-purpose flour, baking powder, and salt in a bowl.
7. When the butter is soft, add the sugar and beat them in a different bowl until the mixture is light and fluffy.

8. Adding the eggs one at a time and mixing them in is the next step.
9. As you add the dry ingredients to the butter mixture, do so in two steps: first, add the dry ingredients, then the pineapple juice, and finally, the milk. Don't mix any further than that.
10. Spread the pineapple slices in the baking pan as you pour the cake batter.
11. After the oven is hot, bake it for 40 to 45 minutes or until a toothpick stuck in the middle comes out clean.
12. Take a short break and let the Pineapple Upside-Down Cake cool in the pan.
13. While the cake is still warm, flip it onto a serving plate so the pineapple topping is on top.
14. Let your Pineapple Upside-Down Cake cool, or serve it warm.

CUBAN BREAD PUDDING (PUDIN DE PAN):

INGREDIENTS:

- 6 cups stale Cuban bread, cut into cubes
- 3 cups whole milk
- 1 cup granulated sugar
- 4 large eggs
- 1 tsp vanilla extract
- 1/2 tsp ground cinnamon
- 1/4 cup raisins (optional)
- 1/4 cup unsalted butter, melted

- Whipped cream and cinnamon for garnish (optional)

Instructions:

1. Warm the oven up to 175°F (350°F). Prepare a 9x13-inch baking dish by greasing it.
2. In a big bowl, mix the bread cubes.
3. Mix the milk, sugar, eggs, vanilla extract, and ground cinnamon in a different bowl using a whisk.
4. Mix the milk and salt, then add the bread cubes. Let them soak for 15 minutes. If you want, add raisins.
5. Add the melted butter to the bread batter and mix it all.
6. Spread the mixture out evenly in the baking dish that has been prepared.
7. It should be baked in a hot oven for 45 to 50 minutes or until the top is golden brown and the pudding is set.
8. You can serve it warm with whipped cream and a sprinkle of cinnamon on top.

COCADA CUBANA (CUBAN COCONUT CANDY):

INGREDIENTS:

- 2 cups shredded coconut
- 1 cup granulated sugar
- 1/2 cup water
- 1/4 tsp vanilla extract
- Pinch of salt

Instructions:

1. Put the sugar, water, and a pinch of salt in a pot. On medium heat, stir the sugar until it melts.
2. After you add the chopped coconut, stir the mixture while cooking until it gets thicker and starts to pull away from the pan's sides.
3. Taking it off the heat, add the vanilla extract and mix it in.
4. Put spoonfuls of the coconut mix on a baking sheet lined with parchment paper or into candy molds.
5. Take the coconut candy out of the fridge and let it cool down. This will help it harden.
6. Once it's hard, take it off the sheet or mold and put it in a container that won't let air in.

CHOCOLATE BABKA WITH RUM GLAZE:

INGREDIENTS: For the Dough:

- 4 cups all-purpose flour
- 1/2 cup granulated sugar
- 1 tsp salt
- 2 1/4 tsp active dry yeast
- 1/2 cup warm milk
- 4 large eggs
- 1 tsp vanilla extract
- 1 cup unsalted butter, softened For the Chocolate Filling:

- 1/2 cup unsalted butter, melted
- 1/2 cup granulated sugar
- 1/2 cup unsweetened cocoa powder
- 1/4 cup dark chocolate chips
- 1/4 cup semisweet chocolate chips For the Rum Glaze:
- 1/2 cup powdered sugar
- 1-2 tbsp dark rum
- 1-2 tbsp milk

Instructions: For the Dough:

1. Combine the all-purpose flour, granulated sugar, and salt in a mixing bowl.
2. In a separate bowl, dissolve the active dry yeast in warm milk and let it sit for about 5 minutes or until foamy.
3. In another bowl, whisk together the eggs and vanilla extract.
4. Gradually add the yeast and egg mixture to the dry ingredients, mixing until a dough forms.
5. Add the softened unsalted butter and knead the dough until it becomes smooth and elastic.
6. Cover the dough and let it rise in a warm place for about 1-2 hours or until doubled in size.
7. For the Chocolate Filling: 7. In a bowl, combine the melted unsalted butter, granulated sugar, and unsweetened cocoa powder to make a chocolate paste.
8. On a floured surface, roll out the dough into a large rectangle.
9. Spread the chocolate paste evenly over the dough, leaving a border around the edges.
10. Sprinkle the dark chocolate chips and semisweet chocolate chips over the chocolate paste.
11. Roll up the dough tightly from the long side to form a log.

12. Cut the log in half lengthwise, exposing the layers of chocolate and dough.
13. Twist the two halves together to create a braided effect.
14. Place the twisted dough into a greased and floured loaf pan.
15. Let the dough rise in the pan for about 30 minutes or until slightly puffed.
16. To Bake: 16. Preheat your oven to 350°F (175°C).
17. Bake the Chocolate Babka in the oven for about 30-35 minutes, or until it's golden brown and sounds hollow when tapped on the bottom.
18. Remove from the oven and let it cool in the pan for a few minutes before transferring it to a wire rack to cool completely.
19. For the Rum Glaze: 19. In a bowl, whisk together the powdered sugar, dark rum, and milk until you reach your desired glaze consistency.
20. Drizzle the rum glaze over the cooled Chocolate Babka.
21. Slice and serve.

GUAVA AND CHEESE STUFFED FRENCH TOAST:

INGREDIENTS:

- 8 slices of bread (such as Cuban bread or French bread)
- 4 oz cream cheese, softened
- 1/2 cup guava paste, softened and diced
- 4 large eggs

- 1/2 cup milk
- 1 tsp vanilla extract
- 1/4 tsp ground cinnamon
- Butter for cooking
- Powdered sugar for dusting (optional)
- Maple syrup for serving (optional)

Instructions:

1. On four slices of bread, spread softened cream cheese. On the other four slices, spread guava paste.
2. Cover one slice of bread with cream cheese and one with guava paste to make 4 sandwiches.
3. The eggs, milk, vanilla extract, and ground cinnamon should all be mixed in a small dish.
4. Spoon or spread some butter into a pan and set it over medium-high heat.
5. Spread out the sandwiches and dip each one into the egg mix. Let each side soak for a short time.
6. While the pan is hot, put the dipped sandwiches on it and cook them until both sides are golden brown and the filling is warm and just a little melted.
7. Take them off the heat and let them cool down a bit.
8. You can serve it with maple syrup and powdered sugar if you want.

MANGO COCONUT POPSICLES:

INGREDIENTS:

- 2 ripe mangoes, peeled and diced
- 1/2 cup coconut milk
- 1/4 cup granulated sugar
- 1/2 tsp vanilla extract
- 1/2 cup shredded coconut (optional)

Instructions:

1. Dice the mangoes with coconut milk, sugar, and vanilla extract in a mixer.
2. Mix until it's smooth.
3. If you want to add more texture, stir in the shredded coconut.
4. Put the fruit and coconut mix into popsicle molds.
5. Put in the popsicle sticks and freeze until solid, which generally takes between 4 and 6 hours or overnight.
6. Take the popsicles out of the pans and serve after they have frozen.

CARAMELIZED PLANTAIN CAKE:

INGREDIENTS:

- 2 ripe plantains, peeled and sliced
- 1/2 cup unsalted butter
- 1/2 cup granulated sugar
- 2 large eggs
- 1 tsp vanilla extract
- 1 1/2 cups all-purpose flour
- 1 1/2 tsp baking powder

- 1/4 tsp salt
- Caramel sauce for drizzling (optional)

Instructions:

1. Warm the oven to 175°F (350°F)—butter and flour in a cake pan.
2. Melt the unsalted butter over low heat in a pot.
3. To the heated butter, add the sliced plantains and sugar. It will take about 10 to 15 minutes of cooking, stirring now and then, until the plantains are soft and browned.
4. Take it off the heat and let it cool down a bit.
5. Beat the eggs in a bowl, add the vanilla extract and mix well.
6. Slowly add the all-purpose flour, baking powder, and salt to the egg mixture until everything is mixed.
7. Add the plantains that have been browned.
8. The cake pan should be ready, so pour the plantain cake batter into it.
9. After the oven is hot, bake it for 30 to 35 minutes or until a toothpick stuck in the middle comes out clean.
10. Caramelized Plantain Cake should cool in the pan for a few minutes before being moved to a wire rack to cool down.
11. If you want, drizzle with caramel sauce before serving.

CUBAN COFFEE CHOCOLATE MOUSSE:

INGREDIENTS:

- 1/2 cup heavy cream
- 1/2 cup Cuban coffee (strongly brewed and cooled)
- 6 oz semisweet chocolate, chopped
- 3 large egg yolks
- 1/4 cup granulated sugar
- 1/4 tsp salt
- 1 cup heavy cream, whipped

Instructions:

1. Put the Cuban coffee and 1/2 cup of heavy cream in a pot. Heat them over medium-low heat until they're hot but not boiling.
2. Take it off the heat and add the chopped semisweet chocolate. After one minute, stir it with a whisk until it's smooth.
3. The egg yolks, powdered sugar, and salt should all be mixed well in a different bowl.
4. Pour the chocolate mixture into the egg yolk mixture slowly to keep the eggs from mixing.
5. Put the mixture back in the pot. Cook it over low heat, stirring it all the time, for about 5 minutes or until it gets thicker. Do not let it get too hot.
6. Leave it alone until it's cool enough to touch.
7. When it's cool, add the whipped cream and mix it in well.
8. Pour the Cuban Coffee Chocolate Mousse into glasses or plates that can hold it.
9. Please put it in the fridge for at least two hours or until it sets.
10. Serve cold.

GUAVA AND CREAM CHEESE OAT BARS:

INGREDIENTS: For the Oat Base and Crumb:

- 1 1/2 cups old-fashioned rolled oats
- 1 1/2 cups all-purpose flour
- 1 cup granulated sugar
- 1/4 tsp baking powder
- 1/4 tsp salt
- 1 cup unsalted butter, melted
- 1 tsp vanilla extract For the Filling:
- 8 oz cream cheese, softened
- 1/2 cup granulated sugar
- 1 large egg
- 1 tsp vanilla extract
- 1/2 cup guava paste, softened and diced

Instructions: For the Oat Base and Crumb:

1. Warm the oven up to 175°F (350°F). Prepare a 9x13-inch baking dish by greasing it.
2. Mix the all-purpose flour, granulated sugar, baking powder, and salt in a bowl.
3. Add the vanilla extract and melted unsalted butter, and mix the ingredients until the dough is crumbly.
4. Press half of the mix into the baking dish that has been greased.
5. To make the filling: 5. When the cream cheese is soft, add the sugar, egg, and vanilla extract to another bowl and beat them together until the mixture is smooth.

6. Spread the cream cheese mix on the baking dish's oat base.
7. Put small amounts of the melted guava paste on the cream cheese layer.
8. Spread the rest of the oat mixture evenly on the fruit layer.
9. For baking: 9. Heat the oven to 350°F. Bake for 30 to 35 minutes until the sides are golden brown and the middle is set.
10. The Guava and Cream Cheese Oat Bars should cool in the dish before they are cut into bars.

TAMARIND SORBET:

INGREDIENTS:

- 2 cups tamarind pulp (from fresh tamarind pods or tamarind paste)
- 1 cup water
- 1/2 cup granulated sugar
- 1/4 cup freshly squeezed lime juice

Instructions:

1. Remove the seeds and strings from the pulp if the tamarind pods are fresh.
2. Put the powdered sugar, water, and tamarind pulp in a saucepan.

3. Stir the mixture constantly over medium-low heat until the sugar melts and the tamarind pulp is thoroughly mixed.
4. Leave it alone until it's cool enough to touch.
5. Add the lime juice that was just squeezed.
6. Put the tamarind mixture into an ice cream maker and churn it as directed by the maker's maker.
7. Put the tamarind sorbet in a jar that won't let air in. Freeze for a few hours or until it's firm.
8. Serve cold.

COCONUT BREAD PUDDING:

INGREDIENTS:

- 6 cups cubed stale Cuban or French bread
- 1 can (13.5 oz) coconut milk
- 1 can (14 oz) sweetened condensed milk
- 4 large eggs
- 1 tsp vanilla extract
- 1/4 cup shredded coconut
- Caramel sauce for drizzling (optional)

Instructions:

1. Warm the oven up to 175°F (350°F). Prepare a baking dish by greasing it.
2. Put the old bread cubes in the baking dish that has been greased.

3. Mix the sweetened condensed milk and coconut milk in a pot. Over medium heat, warm it up, but don't boil it.
4. Take it off the heat and let it cool down a bit.
5. Beat the eggs in a bowl, add the vanilla extract and mix well.
6. Mix the milk mixture into the egg mixture slowly while whisking it in.
7. Put the custard mix on top of the bread cubes in the baking dish. Make sure the bread is thoroughly wet by gently pressing it down.
8. Sprinkle the top with coconut flakes.
9. Warm the oven up and put the bread pudding in it. Bake it for 45 to 50 minutes until it sets and the top is golden brown.
10. Before you serve the Coconut Bread Pudding, let it cool down for a few minutes.
11. If you want, drizzle with caramel sauce.

CHOCOLATE COCONUT RICE PUDDING:

INGREDIENTS:

- 1 cup Arborio rice
- 1 can (13.5 oz) coconut milk
- 4 cups whole milk
- 1/2 cup granulated sugar
- 1/4 cup unsweetened cocoa powder
- 1/2 cup semisweet chocolate chips

- 1 tsp vanilla extract
- Shredded coconut for garnish (optional)

Instructions:

1. Mix the Arborio rice, coconut milk, whole milk, sugar, and unsweetened cocoa powder in a pot.
2. Stir the mixture over medium-low heat until it starts to boil.
3. Turn down the heat and keep cooking, stirring often, for another 20 to 25 minutes, or until the rice is soft and the sauce gets thick.
4. Add the vanilla extract and semisweet chocolate chips and mix them in until the chocolate melts and everything is well mixed.
5. Take it off the heat and let it cool down a bit.
6. You can serve the Chocolate Coconut Rice Pudding warm or cold; if you want, you can top it with chopped coconut.

GUAVA AND CHEESE QUESADILLAS:

INGREDIENTS:

- 4 large flour tortillas
- 1/2 cup guava paste, softened and diced
- 1/2 cup cream cheese, softened
- Butter for cooking

Instructions:

1. Place two of the flour tortillas on the table.

2. Cover the rolls with the softened cream cheese.
3. Put the guava paste dices on top of the cream cheese.
4. Put the last two flour tortillas on top to make quesadilla sandwiches.
5. Put the pan on medium heat and melt some butter in it.
6. In the pan, cook the quesadillas until both sides are golden brown and the filling is warm and just starting to melt.
7. Take them off the heat and let them cool down a bit.
8. Cut it into pieces and serve.

CUBAN CHOCOLATE TIRAMISU:

INGREDIENTS:

- 1 cup strong Cuban coffee, cooled
- 1/4 cup dark rum
- 4 large egg yolks
- 1/2 cup granulated sugar
- 8 oz mascarpone cheese
- 1 cup heavy cream
- 1 tsp vanilla extract
- 1/4 cup unsweetened cocoa powder
- 1 package ladyfingers (about 24)
- Dark chocolate shavings for garnish (optional)

Instructions:

1. Put the iced Cuban coffee and dark rum in a shallow dish.

2. Whisk the egg whites and sugar in a bowl that can handle heat.
3. Put the bowl over a pot of boiling water to make a double boiler. Whisk the mixture all the time until it gets thick and pale, which should take about 5 to 7 minutes.
4. Leave it alone until it's cool enough to touch.
5. Mix the mascarpone cheese into the egg yolk liquid that has been set.
6. Mix the heavy cream and vanilla extract in a different bowl and beat them together until stiff peaks form.
7. Mix the mascarpone and whipped cream slowly until the mixture is smooth.
8. For a few seconds, dip each ladyfinger into the coffee-rum mix. This will let them soak without getting too mushy.
9. Put a layer of wet ladyfingers at the bottom of a dish to serve.
10. Add half of the mascarpone mixture to the ladyfingers and spread it out.
11. Add another layer of wet ladyfingers and the rest of the mascarpone mixture.
12. Pour the chocolate powder that hasn't been sweetened over the top.
13. The Cuban Chocolate Tiramisu should be put in the fridge for at least 4 hours or overnight with the lid on.
14. If you want, you can add dark chocolate pieces as a garnish before serving.

PINEAPPLE COCONUT TRES LECHES CAKE:

INGREDIENTS: For the Cake:

- 1 1/2 cups all-purpose flour
- 1 tsp baking powder
- 1/2 tsp baking soda
- 1/4 tsp salt
- 1/2 cup unsalted butter, softened
- 1 cup granulated sugar
- 3 large eggs
- 1 tsp vanilla extract
- 1/2 cup canned crushed pineapple, drained
- 1/2 cup shredded coconut
- 1/2 cup buttermilk For the Tres Leches Mixture:
- 1 can (14 oz) sweetened condensed milk
- 1 can (12 oz) evaporated milk
- 1/2 cup coconut milk For the Topping:
- Whipped cream
- Toasted shredded coconut
- Fresh pineapple slices (optional)

Instructions: For the Cake:

1. Warm the oven up to 175°F (350°F). A 9x13-inch baking dish should be greased and floured.
2. Put all-purpose flour, baking powder, baking soda, and salt in a bowl and mix them with a whisk.
3. When the butter is soft, add the sugar and beat them in a different bowl until the mixture is light and fluffy.
4. After adding the vanilla extract, beat the eggs one at a time.
5. Add the coconut shreds and crushed pineapple.

6. Slowly add the dry ingredients to the butter mixture, occasionally mixing them with the buttermilk. Start with the dry ingredients and end with the buttermilk. Don't mix any further than that.
7. Pour the cake batter into the baking dish that has been set up.
8. After the oven is hot, bake it for 25 to 30 minutes, or until a toothpick stuck in the middle comes out clean.
9. Take a break and let the cake cool in the pan.
10. For the mix of Tres Leches: 10. The sweetened condensed milk, evaporated milk, and coconut milk should all be mixed in a bowl using a whisk.
11. To Let the Cake Soak: 11. Use a fork or stick to make holes all over the top of the cake while it is still warm.
12. Pour the tres leches mixture over the warm cake slowly so that it can soak in.
13. Put the cake in the fridge for at least two hours or overnight with the lid on.
14. Number 14 for the topping. Put some whipped cream on the chilled cake before serving it.
15. Add toasted shredded coconut on top.
16. If you want, you can add fresh pineapple pieces as a garnish.

PLANTAIN FRITTERS WITH GUAVA DIPPING SAUCE:

INGREDIENTS: For the Plantain Fritters:

- 2 ripe plantains, peeled and mashed
- 1/4 cup all-purpose flour
- 1/4 cup granulated sugar
- 1/2 tsp ground cinnamon
- 1/4 tsp salt
- Vegetable oil for frying For the Guava Dipping Sauce:
- 1/2 cup guava paste, softened and diced
- 1/4 cup water

Instructions: For the Guava Dipping Sauce:

1. Put the chopped guava paste and water in a saucepan.
2. Stir the mixture over low heat until the guava paste melts and it's smooth.
3. Leave it alone until it's cool enough to touch.
4. For the fried plantains: 4. Mash the ripe plantains and mix them with the all-purpose flour, sugar, ground cinnamon, and salt in a bowl. Mix everything well.
5. Put oil from plants into a pan and heat it over medium-low heat.
6. Put spoonfuls of the plantain mix into the hot oil and use the back of a spoon to flatten them.
7. This should take about two to three minutes per side. Fry the patties until both sides are golden brown and crispy.
8. Take the cakes out of the oil and allow them to drain on paper towels.
9. You can dip the plantain fritters in the guava sauce you serve.

CARAMELIZED BANANA CREPES:

INGREDIENTS: For the Crepes:

- 1 cup all-purpose flour
- 2 large eggs
- 1 1/4 cups whole milk
- 2 tbsp melted unsalted butter
- 1/4 tsp salt
- Butter for cooking For the Caramelized Bananas:
- 2 ripe bananas, sliced
- 1/4 cup granulated sugar
- 1/4 cup unsalted butter
- 2 tbsp dark rum (optional)
- Whipped cream for serving (optional)
- Chopped nuts for garnish (optional)

Instructions: For the Crepes:

1. Put the all-purpose flour, eggs, whole milk, melted unsalted butter, and salt in a mixer. Use a blender to make the batter smooth.
2. Melt a little butter in a nonstick skillet or crepe pan over medium heat.
3. Add a slight crepe batter to the hot pan and swirl it to cover the bottom evenly.
4. For about one to two minutes, cook the crepe until the bottom is golden brown and the corners begin to lift. Turn it over and cook it briefly on the other side.

5. Do it again with the rest of the batter, adding more butter to the pan if needed. Place the cooked crepes in a stack on a plate.
6. For the bananas that have been caramelized: 6. Melt the unsalted butter over medium-low heat in a different pan.
7. Add the powdered sugar and stir until it melts and turns into a caramel.
8. Put the banana slices into the sugar that has been browned. Cook for a few minutes until the bananas are covered in the caramel sauce and become softer.
9. When adding dark rum to the pan, avoid splashing it. Instead, use a long lighter or a match to carefully light it. Allow the fire to go out.
10. Add some of the banana filling that has been caramelized to each crepe.
11. The bananas should be on top of the pancakes.
12. If you want, you can top your Caramelized Banana Crepes with whipped cream and chopped nuts.

GUAVA AND CHEESE MUFFINS:

INGREDIENTS:

- 1 1/2 cups all-purpose flour
- 1/2 cup granulated sugar
- 2 tsp baking powder
- 1/4 tsp salt
- 1/2 cup unsalted butter, melted
- 2 large eggs

- 1/2 cup whole milk
- 1/2 cup guava paste, softened and diced
- 1/2 cup cream cheese, softened and diced

Instructions:

1. Warm the oven up to 190°C (375°F). You can line a muffin tin with paper cups.
2. Mix the all-purpose flour, sugar, baking powder, and salt in a bowl using a whisk.
3. Mix the unsalted butter with the eggs and whole milk in a different bowl.
4. Slowly add the wet ingredients to the dry ones until they are mixed.
5. Add the cream cheese and diced guava juice and mix well.
6. Fill up each muffin pan cup about two-thirds of the way to the top with muffin batter.
7. After the oven is hot, bake the muffins for 18 to 20 minutes, or until a toothpick put into the middle comes out clean.
8. Cool the Guava and Cheese Muffins in the pan for a few minutes, then move them to a wire rack to cool down.

COCONUT CUSTARD FLAN:

INGREDIENTS: For the Caramel:

- 1 cup granulated sugar For the Custard:
- 4 large eggs

- 1 can (14 oz) sweetened condensed milk
- 1 can (13.5 oz) coconut milk
- 1 tsp vanilla extract
- 1/4 tsp salt

Instructions: For the Caramel:

1. Melt the granulated sugar in a skillet over medium-high heat while stirring it constantly. This will make a golden caramel.
2. As soon as possible, pour the caramel into the bottom of a flan shape or a heat-safe dish and swirl it around to cover the whole bottom.
3. To make the custard: 3. Use a blender to mix the giant eggs, coconut milk, vanilla extract, sweetened condensed milk, and salt. Mix until it's smooth.
4. Spread the custard mix on the caramel in the flan dish or shape.
5. To Make the Flan Steam: 5. Put metal foil over the flan mold or dish.
6. Putting the flan shape or dish in a bigger pot or steamer with about an inch of water is a good idea.
7. Put a lid on the bigger pot or steamer.
8. A knife stuck in the middle of the flan should come out clean after 50 to 60 minutes of steaming over medium-low heat. This means that the custard is set.
9. Take the flan out of the oven and let it cool down until it's no longer hot.
10. Put the Coconut Custard Flan in the fridge for at least two hours or overnight after it has cooled down.
11. 11. To serve, run a knife around the flan's edge to get it out of the mold.

12. Place a serving platter on top of the mold, flip it over, and carefully remove it to show the custard covered in caramel.
13. Cut your Coconut Custard Flan into pieces and serve it.

CHOCOLATE COCONUT CUPCAKES:

INGREDIENTS: For the Cupcakes:

- 1 1/2 cups all-purpose flour
- 1/2 cup unsweetened cocoa powder
- 1 1/4 tsp baking powder
- 1/2 tsp baking soda
- 1/4 tsp salt
- 1/2 cup unsalted butter, softened
- 1 cup granulated sugar
- 2 large eggs
- 1 tsp vanilla extract
- 1 cup buttermilk
- 1/2 cup shredded coconut For the Coconut Frosting:
- 1/2 cup unsalted butter, softened
- 4 cups powdered sugar
- 1/4 cup coconut milk
- 1 tsp vanilla extract
- 1/2 cup shredded coconut, toasted (for garnish)

Instructions: For the Cupcakes:

1. Warm your oven to 350°F (175°C) and put cupcake liners in a muffin pan.
2. Gather the all-purpose flour, cocoa powder, baking powder, baking soda, and salt in a bowl. Use a whisk to mix them.
3. When the butter is soft, add the sugar and beat them in a different bowl until the mixture is light and fluffy.
4. After adding the vanilla extract, beat the eggs one at a time.
5. Slowly add the dry ingredients to the butter mixture, mixing them with the buttermilk each time. Start with the dry ingredients and end with the buttermilk. Don't mix any further than that.
6. Add the coconut shreds and mix them in.
7. Fill it with batter about two-thirds of the way to the top of each cupcake pan.
8. After the oven is hot, bake the cupcakes for 18 to 20 minutes, or until a toothpick stuck in the middle comes out clean.
9. Let the cupcakes cool down after taking them out of the oven before filling them.
10. For the frosting made with coconut: 10. Put the softened unsalted butter in a bowl and beat it until it's smooth.
11. Add the powdered sugar, coconut milk, and vanilla extract one at a time while beating the frosting. Keep beating it until it is smooth and fluffy.
12. After the cupcakes have cooled, frost them with the coconut frosting and top them with toasted coconut flakes.

GUAVA AND CREAM CHEESE EMPANADAS:

INGREDIENTS: For the Empanada Dough:

- 2 cups all-purpose flour
- 1/2 tsp salt
- 1/2 cup unsalted butter, cold and cubed
- 1/2 cup ice water For the Filling:
- 1/2 cup guava paste, diced
- 4 oz cream cheese, softened
- 1/4 cup granulated sugar
- 1/2 tsp vanilla extract
- Egg wash (1 egg beaten with 1 tbsp water, for brushing)

Instructions: For the Empanada Dough:

1. Put the all-purpose flour and salt in a bowl and mix them.
2. You can use a pastry cutter or your fingers to work the cold, cubed, unsalted butter into the flour until it looks like small crumbs.
3. A little at a time, add ice water and mix until the dough comes together.
4. Put the dough in the fridge for at least 30 minutes after making a disc out of it.
5. To make the filling: 5. Dice the guava paste and mix it with melted cream cheese, sugar, and vanilla extract in a bowl until everything is well mixed.
6. To Put Together: 6. Warm your oven up to 190°C (375°F) and put parchment paper on a baking sheet.

7. Spread the cold empanada dough on a floured surface until it is about 1/8-inch thick.
8. Cut the dough into circles with a round tool.
9. Put some guava and cream cheese filling in the middle of each dough circle.
10. To make a half-moon shape, fold the dough and press the sides with a fork to seal them.
11. Lay the empanadas out on the baking sheet that has been prepared.
12. Use the egg wash to cover the tops of the empanadas.
13. How to Bake: 13. When the oven is hot, put the empanadas in it for 20 to 25 minutes, or until they turn golden brown.
14. Take them out of the oven and let them cool down before serving them.

GUAVA AND CHEESE DANISH:

INGREDIENTS: For the Danish Dough:

- 1 package (2 1/4 tsp) active dry yeast
- 1/4 cup warm water
- 1/4 cup granulated sugar
- 1/2 cup unsalted butter, softened
- 2 cups all-purpose flour
- 1/4 tsp salt
- 1/2 cup whole milk
- 1 large egg For the Guava and Cheese Filling:
- 1/2 cup guava paste, softened and diced

- 4 oz cream cheese, softened
- 2 tbsp powdered sugar
- 1/2 tsp vanilla extract For the Glaze:
- 1/2 cup powdered sugar
- 1-2 tbsp milk
- 1/2 tsp vanilla extract

Instructions: For the Danish Dough:

1. Put the all-purpose flour and salt in a bowl and mix them.
2. You can use a pastry cutter or your fingers to work the cold, cubed, unsalted butter into the flour until it looks like small crumbs.
3. A little at a time, add ice water and mix until the dough comes together.
4. Put the dough in the fridge for at least 30 minutes after making a disc out of it.
5. To make the filling: 5. Dice the guava paste and mix it with melted cream cheese, sugar, and vanilla extract in a bowl until everything is well mixed.
6. To Put Together: 6. Warm your oven up to 190°C (375°F) and put parchment paper on a baking sheet.
7. Spread the cold empanada dough on a floured surface until it is about 1/8-inch thick.
8. Cut the dough into circles with a round tool.
9. Put some guava and cream cheese filling in the middle of each dough circle.
10. To make a half-moon shape, fold the dough and press the sides with a fork to seal them.
11. Lay the empanadas out on the baking sheet that has been prepared.
12. Use the egg wash to cover the tops of the empanadas.

13. How to Bake: 13. When the oven is hot, put the empanadas in it for 20 to 25 minutes, or until they turn golden brown.
14. Take them out of the oven and let them cool down before serving.

PINEAPPLE RUM CAKE:

INGREDIENTS: For the Cake:

- 2 cups all-purpose flour
- 2 tsp baking powder
- 1/2 tsp baking soda
- 1/4 tsp salt
- 1/2 cup unsalted butter, softened
- 1 cup granulated sugar
- 2 large eggs
- 1 tsp vanilla extract
- 1 cup crushed pineapple, drained
- 1/2 cup rum (dark or light) For the Rum Glaze:
- 1/2 cup unsalted butter
- 1 cup granulated sugar
- 1/4 cup water
- 1/4 cup rum (dark or light)

Instructions: For the Cake:

1. Warm your oven to 175°F (350°C) and grease a bundt cake pan.
2. Put all-purpose flour, baking powder, baking soda, and salt in a bowl and mix them with a whisk.
3. When the butter is soft, add the sugar and beat them in a different bowl until the mixture is light and fluffy.
4. After adding the vanilla extract, beat the eggs one at a time.
5. Slowly add the dry ingredients to the butter mixture until they are mixed.
6. Add the rum and crushed pineapple and mix well.
7. When the bundt cake pan is ready, pour the cake batter into it.
8. How to Bake: 8. After the oven is hot, bake the cake for 35 to 40 minutes, or until a toothpick stuck in the middle comes out clean.
9. Just take the cake out of the oven and let it cool in the pan.
10. These numbers are for the Rum Glaze: 10. While the butter is on medium heat, melt it in a pot.
11. Mix in the water and powdered sugar, then bring the whole thing to a boil.
12. Turn down the heat and stir the food all the time for about 5 minutes.
13. Take it off the heat and add the rum while stirring.
14. To Cover the Cake in Glaze: 14. Use a stick to make holes all over the top of the cake while it is still warm.
15. Pour the rum glaze over the warm cake slowly so that it can soak in.
16. Before you serve the cake, let it cool down.

COCONUT PANNA COTTA:

INGREDIENTS:

- 1 1/2 cups coconut milk
- 1/2 cup whole milk
- 1/2 cup granulated sugar
- 1 tsp vanilla extract
- 2 1/4 tsp unflavored gelatin
- 3 tbsp cold water
- Shredded coconut and fresh berries for garnish (optional)

Instructions:

1. Coconut milk, whole milk, sugar, and vanilla flavor should all be mixed in a saucepan.
2. Stir the mixture over medium-low heat until it's hot but not boiling. Take it off the heat.
3. Spread the plain gelatin over the cold water in a different small bowl. Allow it to grow for about 5 minutes.
4. Add the expanded gelatin to the hot milk mixture and stir until it's all gone.
5. Put the mix into ramekins or panna cotta pans.
6. Please put in the fridge for at least four hours or until it sets.
7. To Give: 7. Spread the Coconut Panna Cotta on plates to serve.
8. You can add shredded coconut and fresh berries as a garnish.

MAMEY SMOOTHIE BOWL:

INGREDIENTS:

- 1 ripe mamey, peeled and seeded
- 1 banana
- 1/2 cup coconut milk
- 1/4 cup Greek yogurt
- 1 tbsp honey (optional)
- Toppings: sliced banana, shredded coconut, chia seeds, granola, and fresh fruit

Instructions:

1. Put the ripe mango, banana, coconut milk, Greek yogurt, and honey (if you want) in a blender.
2. Mix until it's creamy and smooth.
3. Get a bowl and pour the drink in it.
4. Add your pick of fresh fruit, shredded coconut, chia seeds, and sliced banana.
5. Serve your Mamey Smoothie Bowl right away and have fun!

GUAVA AND CREAM CHEESE SCONES:

INGREDIENTS:

- 2 cups all-purpose flour
- 1/4 cup granulated sugar

- 2 tsp baking powder
- 1/2 tsp baking soda
- 1/2 tsp salt
- 1/2 cup unsalted butter, cold and cubed
- 1/2 cup guava paste, diced
- 4 oz cream cheese, cold and cubed
- 1/2 cup buttermilk
- 1 tsp vanilla extract
- 1 egg (for egg wash)
- Additional sugar for sprinkling

Instructions:

1. Warm your oven to 400°F (200°C) and put parchment paper on a baking sheet.
2. Mix the all-purpose flour, sugar, baking powder, baking soda, and salt in a bowl using a whisk to make the dough.
3. Add the cold, cubed, unsalted butter to the dry ingredients. Cut the butter into the flour with a pastry cutter or your fingers until the mixture resembles big crumbs.
4. Add the cream cheese and diced guava juice and mix well.
5. Add the buttermilk and vanilla extract to a different bowl and mix them using a whisk.
6. Slowly add the buttermilk mixture to the dough and mix it in until it's just mixed.
7. Put the dough on a greased surface and knead it a few times to bring it all together.
8. Make a circle out of the dough that is about an inch thick.
9. Make 8 pieces out of the dough.
10. To make the egg wash: 10. Beat the egg in a small bowl.
11. Spread the beaten egg on the scones and then sprinkle with more sugar.

12. How to Bake: 12. Put the scones on the baking sheet that has been prepared.
13. Heat the oven and put the scones in it. Bake for 15 to 18 minutes, or until they turn golden brown.
14. Take them out of the oven and let them cool down before serving them.

CUBAN COFFEE CHOCOLATE CHIP COOKIES:

INGREDIENTS:

- 1 cup unsalted butter, softened
- 1 cup granulated sugar
- 1/2 cup brown sugar, packed
- 2 large eggs
- 2 tbsp Cuban coffee (strong brewed coffee works too)
- 2 tsp vanilla extract
- 2 1/2 cups all-purpose flour
- 1 tsp baking soda
- 1/2 tsp salt
- 2 cups semisweet chocolate chips

Instructions:

1. Warm the oven to 350°F (175°C) and put parchment paper on a baking sheet.
2. Mix the unsalted butter with powdered and brown sugar in a bowl until light and fluffy.

3. The Cuban coffee (strong made coffee) and vanilla extract come next. Beat in the eggs one at a time.
4. Mix the all-purpose flour, baking soda, and salt in a different bowl.
5. Slowly add the dry ingredients to the wet ones until they are mixed.
6. Add the semisweet chocolate chips and mix them in.
7. Place cookie dough spoonfuls on the baking sheet that has been prepared, leaving about 2 inches between each one.
8. How to Bake: 8. Place the cookies in an oven that has already been heated. Bake for 10 to 12 minutes or until the sides are golden brown and the centers are set.
9. After taking the cookies out of the oven, let them cool for a few minutes on the baking sheet before moving them to a wire rack.

PLANTAIN AND COCONUT TARTS:

INGREDIENTS: For the Tart Crust:

- 1 1/4 cups all-purpose flour
- 1/4 cup granulated sugar
- 1/4 tsp salt
- 1/2 cup unsalted butter, cold and cubed
- 1 large egg yolk
- 1-2 tbsp ice water For the Plantain and Coconut Filling:
- 2 ripe plantains, peeled and diced
- 1/2 cup shredded coconut
- 1/2 cup coconut milk

- 1/4 cup granulated sugar
- 1/4 tsp ground cinnamon
- 1/4 tsp vanilla extract
- Pinch of salt
- Unsweetened coconut flakes (for garnish)

Instructions: For the Tart Crust:

1. Use a food processor to combine all-purpose flour, sugar, and salt.
2. Add the unsalted, cold butter cubes and pulse the mixture until it looks like coarse bits.
3. Add the egg yolk and 1 tablespoon of ice water to a small bowl and mix them using a whisk.
4. Slowly add the egg yolk mixture to the food processor while running until the dough comes together. One teaspoon at a time, add more ice water if you need to.
5. Put the dough in the fridge for at least 30 minutes after making a disc out of it.
6. To make the filling of plantain and coconut: 6. Diced ripe plantains, shredded coconut, coconut milk, sugar, ground cinnamon, vanilla extract, and a pinch of salt should all be put in a pot.
7. Stir the mixture over medium heat for 10 to 15 minutes or until it thickens and the plantains softens.
8. Take it off the heat and let it cool down a bit.
9. 9. Preheat your oven to 350°F (175°C) before compiling it.
10. Roll out the cold tart dough on a floured surface to fit tart pans or a tart pan with a bottom that can be removed.
11. Put the dough into the tart pan(s) and cut off any extra.
12. Mix the plantain and coconut and pour them into the tart shell(s).

13. 13. Put the tart in an oven that has already been heated for 25 to 30 minutes or until the top is golden brown.
14. Take the tarts out of the oven and let them cool down until they're not hot!
15. To add the garnish: 15. In a dry pan over medium-low heat, toast coconut flakes without sugar until they turn golden brown.
16. Put toasted coconut flakes on top of the tarts after they have cooled.

GUAVA AND CHEESE STUFFED CREPES:

INGREDIENTS: For the Crepes:

- 1 cup all-purpose flour
- 2 large eggs
- 1 1/4 cups whole milk
- 2 tbsp melted unsalted butter
- 1/4 tsp salt
- Butter for cooking For the Guava and Cheese Filling:
- 1/2 cup guava paste, softened and diced
- 4 oz cream cheese, softened

Instructions: For the Crepes:

1. Put the all-purpose flour, eggs, whole milk, melted unsalted butter, and salt in a mixer. Use a blender to make the batter smooth.
2. Melt a little butter in a nonstick skillet or crepe pan over medium heat.
3. Add a slight crepe batter to the hot pan and swirl it to cover the bottom evenly.
4. For about one to two minutes, cook the crepe until the bottom is golden brown and the corners begin to lift. Turn it over and cook it briefly on the other side.
5. Do it again with the rest of the batter, adding more butter to the pan if needed. Place the cooked crepes in a stack on a plate.
6. For the filling of guava and cheese: 6. Put the softened cream cheese and diced guava paste in a bowl until they are well mixed.
7. To Put Together: 7. Put a little of the guava and cheese filling on each crepe.
8. To make a half-moon form, fold the crepes over.

CARAMELIZED MANGO WITH COCONUT CREAM:

INGREDIENTS:

- 2 ripe mangoes, peeled and sliced
- 1/4 cup granulated sugar
- 2 tbsp unsalted butter
- 1/4 cup coconut milk

- Toasted coconut flakes for garnish (optional)

Instructions:

1. Melt the unsalted butter over medium-low heat in a pan.
2. Add the powdered sugar and stir until it melts and turns into a caramel.
3. Add the sliced mangoes to the sugar that has been caramelized. Cook for a few minutes until the mangoes are covered in the caramel sauce and have become softer.
4. Take it off the heat and let it cool down a bit.
5. For the cream of coconut: 5. Mix the coconut milk with a whisk in a different bowl until it is smooth.
6. To Give: 6. Pour the coconut cream over the sautéed mango slices.
7. If you want, you can top it off with toasted coconut bits.

CHOCOLATE COCONUT MOUSSE:

INGREDIENTS:

- 6 oz semisweet chocolate, chopped
- 1/4 cup unsalted butter
- 1/4 cup strong brewed coffee
- 3 large eggs, separated
- 1/4 cup granulated sugar
- 1 tsp vanilla extract
- 1 cup coconut milk
- Shredded coconut and chocolate shavings for garnish (optional)

Instructions:

1. Put the chopped semisweet chocolate, unsalted butter, and strong-made coffee in a heatproof bowl.
2. Double-boil the water in a pot and set the bowl over it. Stir the mixture until the butter and chocolate are melted and smooth. Take it off the heat and let it cool down a bit.
3. Mix the egg whites, sugar, and vanilla extract in a different bowl with a whisk until everything is well blended.
4. Whisk the egg yolk mixture into the melted chocolate mixture gradually until the mixture is smooth.
5. Beat the egg whites in a different bowl until they make stiff peaks.
6. Mix the egg whites into the chocolate mixture slowly until thoroughly combined.
7. Lightly beat the coconut milk until it becomes fluffy.
8. Fold the whipped coconut milk into the chocolate mixture slowly until everything is well mixed.
9. Pour the chocolate coconut mousse into glasses or plates that can be used to serve it.
10. Please put it in the fridge for at least two hours or until it sets.
11. For the garnish: 11. If you want, decorate it before serving with shredded coconut and chocolate bits.

GUAVA AND CREAM CHEESE PARFAIT:

INGREDIENTS:

- 1/2 cup guava paste, softened and diced
- 4 oz cream cheese, softened
- 1 cup Greek yogurt
- 2 tbsp honey
- Granola for layering
- Fresh guava slices for garnish (optional)

Instructions:

1. Put the softened cream cheese and diced guava paste in a bowl and mix them until they are well mixed.
2. Mix the Greek yogurt and honey in a different bowl with a whisk until smooth.
3. Put the guava, cream cheese, Greek yogurt, and granola in serving cups or bowls.
4. If you want, you can repeat the layers.
5. If you want, you can add fresh guava pieces as a garnish.

PINEAPPLE COCONUT MACADAMIA NUT BARS:

INGREDIENTS: For the Crust:

- 1 1/2 cups graham cracker crumbs
- 1/2 cup unsalted butter, melted For the Filling:
- 1 can (20 oz) crushed pineapple, drained
- 2 cups shredded coconut

- 1 cup macadamia nuts, chopped
- 1 can (14 oz) sweetened condensed milk
- 1/4 cup lemon juice
- 1 tsp vanilla extract

Instructions: For the Crust:

1. Warm the oven to 350°F (175°C) and put parchment paper in a 9x13-inch baking pan.
2. Mix the graham cracker crumbs and hot unsalted butter in a bowl.
3. Spread the mix out in the bottom of the baking pan that has been prepped.
4. To make the filling: 4. Put the drained crushed pineapple, grated coconut, chopped macadamia nuts, sweetened condensed milk, lemon juice, and vanilla extract in a bowl.
5. Mix the items until they are well mixed.
6. Spread the liquid out evenly over the crust in the baking pan.
7. How to Bake: 7. Place the pan in an oven that has already been heated. Bake the bars for 25 to 30 minutes until they are set and the edges are golden brown.
8. Remove them from the oven and leave them in the pan to cool down.

TRES LECHES FLAN:

INGREDIENTS: For the Tres Leches Cake:

- 1 1/2 cups all-purpose flour
- 1 1/2 tsp baking powder
- 1/4 tsp salt
- 1/2 cup unsalted butter, softened
- 1 cup granulated sugar
- 5 large eggs
- 1 tsp vanilla extract
- 1/2 cup whole milk
- 1/2 cup evaporated milk
- 1/2 cup sweetened condensed milk For the Flan:
- 1 can (14 oz) sweetened condensed milk
- 1 can (12 oz) evaporated milk
- 4 large eggs
- 1 tsp vanilla extract

Instructions: For the Tres Leches Cake:

1. Warm the oven up to 175°F (350°F). Prepare a 9x13-inch baking dish by greasing it.
2. Whisk the all-purpose flour, baking powder, and salt in a bowl.
3. Beat the unsalted butter and powdered sugar until light and fluffy in a different bowl.
4. After adding the vanilla extract, beat the eggs one at a time.
5. Slowly add the dry ingredients to the butter mixture and mix them until they are mixed.
6. Add the whole milk and mix it in.
7. After preparing the baking dish, pour the cake batter into it and spread it evenly.

8. How to Make Flan: 8. Put the evaporated milk, eggs, vanilla extract, and sweetened condensed milk in a mixer. Mix until it's smooth.
9. Pour the flan mixture over the cake batter in the baking dish slowly.
10. Ten things to bake. After the oven is hot, bake it for 45 to 50 minutes, or until a toothpick stuck in the middle comes out clean.
11. Take it out of the oven and let it cool down until it's even.
12. Put the Tres Leches Flan in the fridge for at least two hours before you serve it.

GUAVA AND CHEESE PALMIERS:

INGREDIENTS:

- 1 sheet puff pastry, thawed
- 1/2 cup guava paste, softened and diced
- 4 oz cream cheese, softened

Instructions:

1. Warm your oven to 400°F (200°C) and put parchment paper on a baking sheet.
2. Put some flour on a table and roll the puff pastry sheet into a rectangle shape.
3. Cover the puff pastry with the melted guava paste.
4. The melted cream cheese should be spread on top of the guava paste.
5. Roll the puff pastry into a tight log starting at one end.

6. Cut the log into pieces that are 1/2 inch thick.
7. How to Bake: 7. Place the rounds of palmiers on the baking sheet that has been prepared.
8. After the hot oven, bake the palmiers for 15 to 20 minutes or until golden brown and puffy.
9. Take them out of the oven and let them cool down before serving them.

COCONUT RUM TRIFLE:

INGREDIENTS: For the Cake Layer:

- 1 store-bought sponge cake or pound cake, cut into cubes
- 1/4 cup dark rum For the Coconut Cream Layer:
- 1 can (13.5 oz) coconut milk
- 1 cup heavy cream
- 1/2 cup granulated sugar
- 1 tsp coconut extract For the Whipped Cream Layer:
- 1 cup heavy cream
- 2 tbsp powdered sugar
- Shredded coconut and toasted coconut flakes for garnish (optional)

Instructions: For the Cake Layer:

1. Put the pieces of sponge cake or pound cake in a trifle dish.
2. Pour the dark rum over the cake cubes in a thin layer.

3. To make the layer of coconut cream: 3. Put the coconut milk, heavy cream, sugar, and coconut flavor in a saucepan and mix them.
4. Stir the mixture constantly over medium-low heat until it's hot but not boiling.
5. Take it off the heat and let it cool down a bit.
6. Spread the coconut cream mix on top of the cake layer in the dessert dish.
7. 1. For the layer of whipped cream: 7. Heavy cream and powdered sugar should be whipped together in a bowl until stiff peaks form.
8. Add the whipped cream on top of the coconut cream.
9. To Decorate: 9. If you want, you can decorate the Coconut Rum Trifle with toasted coconut flakes and coconut shreds.
10. Please put it in the fridge for at least two hours before you serve it.

CINNAMON SUGAR PLANTAIN EMPANADAS:

INGREDIENTS: For the Empanada Dough:

- 2 cups all-purpose flour
- 1/2 tsp salt
- 1/2 cup unsalted butter, cold and cubed
- 1/2 cup ice water For the Cinnamon Sugar Plantain Filling:

- 2 ripe plantains, peeled and sliced
- 1/4 cup granulated sugar
- 1 tsp ground cinnamon
- Vegetable oil for frying For the Cinnamon Sugar Coating:
- 1/4 cup granulated sugar
- 1 tsp ground cinnamon

Instructions: For the Empanada Dough:

1. Put the all-purpose flour and salt in a bowl and mix them.
2. You can use a pastry cutter or your fingers to work the cold, cubed, unsalted butter into the flour until it looks like small crumbs.
3. A little at a time, add ice water and mix until the dough comes together.
4. Put the dough in the fridge for at least 30 minutes after making a disc out of it.
5. What you need for the cinnamon sugar plantain filling: 5. Sliced ripe plantains, sugar, and ground cinnamon should all be put in a bowl together. Toss the plantains to cover them all over.
6. To Put Together: 6. Warm the oven up to 350°F (175°C) and put parchment paper on a baking sheet.
7. Spread the cold empanada dough on a floured surface until it is about 1/8-inch thick.
8. Use a round cutter to make rings out of the dough.
9. Put some of the plantain filling with cinnamon and sugar in the middle of each dough circle.
10. To make a half-moon shape, fold the dough and press the sides with a fork to seal them.
11. In a large pan or skillet, heat the vegetable oil to 350°F (175°C).

12. Twelve to fry. Add the plantain empanadas to the hot oil a few at a time and fry them until both sides are golden brown.
13. Take it out of the oil and let it drain on paper towels.
14. It takes 14 for the cinnamon sugar coating. Put the cinnamon powder and powdered sugar in a bowl and mix them.
15. Roll the plantain empanadas in the cinnamon sugar mixture to cover them all the way through while they are still warm.

MAMEY CHEESECAKE:

INGREDIENTS: For the Crust:

- 1 1/2 cups graham cracker crumbs
- 1/4 cup granulated sugar
- 1/2 cup unsalted butter, melted For the Mamey Cheesecake Filling:
- 3 cups ripe mamey, peeled and mashed
- 24 oz cream cheese, softened
- 1 1/2 cups granulated sugar
- 4 large eggs
- 1 tsp vanilla extract For the Mamey Glaze (optional):
- 1 cup ripe mamey, peeled and mashed
- 1/4 cup granulated sugar

Instructions: For the Crust:

1. Warm the oven to 325°F (160°C) and grease a 9-inch springform pan.
2. Mix the graham cracker crumbs, sugar, and melted unsalted butter in a bowl.
3. Fill the bottom of the springform pan with the filling and press it down.
4. For the filling of the Mamey cheesecake: 4. Soften the cream cheese and beat it in a bowl until it is smooth and creamy.
5. Mix in the powdered sugar by beating it in well.
6. Mix in the mashed ripe mamey and keep beating until the mixture is smooth.
7. After adding the vanilla extract, beat the eggs one at a time.
8. Put the base in the springform pan and then pour the mamey cheesecake filling on top of it.
9. For baking: 9. For about 60 to 70 minutes, or until the sides of the cheesecake are set but the middle is still wobbly, bake it in a hot oven.
10. Leave the oven door open for about an hour and turn off the heat. This will help the cheesecake cool down slowly.
11. After taking the cheesecake out of the oven, put it in the fridge for at least 4 hours or until it is freezing.
12. Optional: For the Mamey Glaze: 12. Mix the ripe mamey with the powdered sugar in a saucepan.
13. Stir the mixture while cooking over low heat until it turns into a sauce.
14. Could you wait for it to cool down?
15. To Give: 15. If you are using it, drizzle the mamey sauce over the chilled cheesecake right before serving.

GUAVA AND CHEESE STUFFED WAFFLES:

INGREDIENTS: For the Waffle Batter:

- 2 cups all-purpose flour
- 2 tbsp granulated sugar
- 1 tbsp baking powder
- 1/2 tsp salt
- 2 large eggs
- 1 3/4 cups milk
- 1/2 cup unsalted butter, melted
- 1 tsp vanilla extract For the Guava and Cheese Filling:
- 1/2 cup guava paste, softened and diced
- 4 oz cream cheese, softened
- Maple syrup for serving

Instructions: For the Waffle Batter:

1. Follow the directions that came with your waffle pan to get it hot.
2. Mix the all-purpose flour, sugar, baking powder, and salt in a bowl using a whisk.
3. Now, put the eggs in a different bowl and beat them. Then add the milk, melted unsalted butter, and vanilla extract. Mix everything well.
4. Add the wet ingredients to the dry ones and mix them just until they are mixed.
5. To fill the pie with guava and cheese: 5. Put the softened cream cheese and diced guava paste in a bowl and mix them until they are well mixed.

6. Steps to Make Stuffed Waffles: 6. Use nonstick food spray to grease the waffle iron.
7. Put some waffle batter on the waffle iron using a spoon.
8. Place a small amount of the guava and cheese filling on the batter.
9. More pancake batter should be put on top to cover the filling.
10. Follow the directions on the waffle iron's box to cook the waffles until they are golden brown and done all the way through.
11. Carefully take the waffles out of the iron that have been stuffed.
12. To Give: 12. Put some maple syrup on top of your Guava and Cheese Stuffed Waffles and eat them.

BANANA AND COCONUT BREAD:

INGREDIENTS:

- 2 cups all-purpose flour
- 1 1/2 tsp baking powder
- 1/2 tsp baking soda
- 1/4 tsp salt
- 1/2 cup unsalted butter, softened
- 1 cup granulated sugar
- 2 large eggs
- 3 ripe bananas, mashed
- 1 tsp vanilla extract
- 1/2 cup shredded coconut

- 1/2 cup chopped walnuts (optional)

Instructions:

1. Warm the oven to 350°F (175°C) and grease a loaf pan.
2. Put all-purpose flour, baking powder, baking soda, and salt in a bowl and mix them with a whisk.
3. Beat the unsalted butter and powdered sugar until light and fluffy in a different bowl.
4. The mashed ripe bananas and vanilla extract should be added after the eggs are beat in one at a time.
5. Slowly add the dry ingredients to the banana mixture and mix them until they are mixed.
6. If you want, you can add the chopped walnuts and crushed coconut.
7. Fill the loaf pan with the banana coconut bread batter.
8. How to Bake: 8. After the oven is hot, bake it for about 60 to 70 minutes, or until a toothpick stuck in the middle comes out clean.
9. Take the pan out of the oven and let the bread cool for a few minutes before moving it to a wire rack to cool through.

CARAMELIZED PAPAYA WITH RUM GLAZE:

INGREDIENTS:

- 1 ripe papaya, peeled, seeded, and sliced
- 1/4 cup granulated sugar

- 2 tbsp unsalted butter
- 1/4 cup dark rum
- Vanilla ice cream for serving (optional)

Instructions:

1. Melt the unsalted butter over medium-low heat in a pan.
2. Add the powdered sugar and stir until it melts and turns into a caramel.
3. Add the papaya slices to the sugar that has been caramelized. Cook for a few minutes until the papaya is covered in the caramel sauce and gets a little softer.
4. Take it off the heat.
5. To make the Rum Glaze: 5. Put the dark rum in a pot and warm it over low heat.
6. To Give: 6. Put the warm rum on top of the papaya that has been toasted.
7. If you want, you can serve the caramelized papaya with vanilla ice cream.

CUBAN COFFEE TRES LECHES CAKE:

INGREDIENTS: For the Cake:

- 1 1/2 cups all-purpose flour
- 1 1/2 tsp baking powder
- 1/4 tsp salt
- 1/2 cup unsalted butter, softened
- 1 cup granulated sugar

- 3 large eggs
- 1 tsp vanilla extract
- 1/2 cup strong brewed Cuban coffee (or strong coffee)
- 1/4 cup whole milk For the Tres Leches:
- 1 can (14 oz) sweetened condensed milk
- 1 can (12 oz) evaporated milk
- 1/2 cup heavy cream
- 1/4 cup strong brewed Cuban coffee (or strong coffee) For the Whipped Cream:
- 1 cup heavy cream
- 2 tbsp powdered sugar
- Cocoa powder for dusting (optional)

Instructions: For the Cake:

1. Warm the oven up to 175°F (350°F). Prepare a 9x13-inch baking dish by greasing it.
2. Whisk the all-purpose flour, baking powder, and salt in a bowl.
3. Beat the unsalted butter and powdered sugar until light and fluffy in a different bowl.
4. After adding the vanilla extract, beat the eggs one at a time.
5. Slowly add the dry ingredients to the butter mixture and mix them until they are mixed.
6. Add the strong coffee (or Cuban coffee) that has been made and whole milk.
7. After preparing the baking dish, pour the cake batter into it and spread it evenly.
8. How to Make Tres Leches: 8. Put the heavy cream, sweetened condensed milk, evaporated milk, and strong

made Cuban coffee (or strong coffee) in a bowl and mix them using a whisk.
9. Use your hands to spread the tres leches mixture over the warm cake.
10. For about 30 minutes, let the cake soak up the water.
11. To make the whipped cream: 11. Heavy and powdered sugar should be whipped together in a bowl until stiff peaks form.
12. Cover the cake with the whipped cream.
13. To Serve: 13. If you want, sprinkle cocoa powder on top of the Cuban Coffee Tres Leches Cake.
14. Please put it in the fridge for at least two hours before you serve it.

PINEAPPLE COCONUT CUPCAKES:

INGREDIENTS: For the Cupcakes:

- 1 1/2 cups all-purpose flour
- 1 1/2 tsp baking powder
- 1/4 tsp salt
- 1/2 cup unsalted butter, softened
- 1 cup granulated sugar
- 2 large eggs
- 1 tsp vanilla extract
- 1/2 cup crushed pineapple, drained
- 1/2 cup shredded coconut
- 1/4 cup pineapple juice (from the canned pineapple) For the Coconut Cream Cheese Frosting:

- 8 oz cream cheese, softened
- 1/2 cup unsalted butter, softened
- 3 cups powdered sugar
- 1/2 cup shredded coconut
- 1 tsp coconut extract
- Additional shredded coconut for garnish (optional)

Instructions: For the Cupcakes:

1. Warm your oven to 350°F (175°C) and put cupcake liners in a muffin pan.
2. Whisk the all-purpose flour, baking powder, and salt in a bowl.
3. Beat the unsalted butter and powdered sugar until light and fluffy in a different bowl.
4. After adding the vanilla extract, beat the eggs one at a time.
5. Slowly add the dry ingredients to the butter mixture and mix them until they are mixed.
6. Mix well with the crushed pineapple, coconut shreds, and pineapple juice.
7. Fill each cupcake pan with an equal amount of cupcake batter.
8. How to Bake: 8. After the oven is hot, bake the cupcakes for 18 to 20 minutes, or until a toothpick stuck in the middle comes out clean.
9. After taking the cupcakes out of the oven, let them cool in the muffin tin for a few minutes. Then, move them to a wire rack to cool fully.
10. Here are the steps for making the coconut cream cheese frosting: 10. Spread melted cream cheese and unsalted butter in a bowl and mix them until they are smooth and creamy.

11. Add the powdered sugar slowly while beating it until it is well mixed.
12. Add the coconut shreds and coconut flavor and mix them in.
13. Frost: 13. Use the Coconut Cream Cheese Frosting to decorate the cupcakes once they are completely cool.
14. If you want, you can add more shredded coconut as a garnish.

MAMEY AND COCONUT SMOOTHIE:

INGREDIENTS:

- 1 ripe mamey, peeled, seeded, and diced
- 1/2 cup coconut milk
- 1/2 cup coconut water
- 1/4 cup honey
- Ice cubes

Instructions:

1. Diced ripe mamey, coconut milk, coconut water, honey, and a few ice cubes should all be put into a mixer.
2. Mix until it's creamy and smooth.
3. The Mamey and Coconut Smoothie should be served right away.

GUAVA AND CHEESE BRIOCHE:

INGREDIENTS: For the Brioche Dough:

- 2 1/4 cups all-purpose flour
- 1/4 cup granulated sugar
- 2 1/4 tsp active dry yeast
- 1/2 tsp salt
- 1/2 cup warm milk
- 2 large eggs
- 1/2 cup unsalted butter, softened For the Guava and Cheese Filling:
- 1/2 cup guava paste, softened and diced
- 4 oz cream cheese, softened For the Egg Wash:
- 1 egg
- 1 tbsp water

Instructions: For the Brioche Dough:

1. Mix the all-purpose flour, sugar, active dry yeast, and salt in a bowl using a whisk.
2. Stir in the warm milk until everything is well mixed.
3. One egg at a time, mixing well after each addition.
4. Add the melted unsalted butter and knead the dough until it is smooth and stretchy. Or, you can knead by hand or use a stand machine with a dough hook.
5. Cover the dough and set it in a buttered bowl. Let it rise in a warm place for one to two hours, or until it goes double in size.
6. 6. Put the diced guava paste and melted cream cheese in a bowl until they are well mixed.

7. To Put Together: 7. Set your oven to 350°F (175°C) and grease a round cake pan or brioche pan.
8. Once the brioche dough has risen, punch it down and cut it into equal pieces.
9. Please make a small circle out of each piece by rolling it out.
10. To Fill and Shape: 10. Put some guava and cheese filling on each circle.
11. To seal the edges, fold the dough to make a half-moon form.
12. 12. Beat the egg and water together in a small bowl for the egg wash.
13. Use the egg wash to cover the bread.
14. To bake: 14. Put the brioche in the oiled pan after it has been filled and shaped.
15. After getting the oven hot, bake the brioche for 20 to 25 minutes or until it's golden brown and done all the way through.
16. Take it out of the oven and let it cool down before serving it.

CHOCOLATE COCONUT BISCOTTI:

INGREDIENTS:

- 2 cups all-purpose flour
- 1/2 cup unsweetened cocoa powder
- 1 1/2 tsp baking powder
- 1/4 tsp salt

- 1/2 cup unsalted butter, softened
- 1 cup granulated sugar
- 2 large eggs
- 1 tsp vanilla extract
- 1/2 cup shredded coconut
- 1/2 cup semisweet chocolate chips

Instructions:

1. Warm the oven up to 350°F (175°C) and put parchment paper on a baking sheet.
2. Whisk the all-purpose flour, cocoa powder, baking powder, and salt in a bowl.
3. Beat the unsalted butter and powdered sugar until light and fluffy in a different bowl.
4. After adding the vanilla extract, beat the eggs one at a time.
5. Slowly add the dry ingredients to the butter mixture and mix them until they are mixed.
6. Add the semisweet chocolate chips and chopped coconut and mix well.
7. Step 7: Split the cookie dough in half.
8. Make a floured log of each half, about 12 inches long and 2 inches wide.
9. To bake: 9. Place the logs on the baking sheet that has been prepared, leaving room between them.
10. Before you put the logs in the oven, heat it. Bake them for 25 to 30 minutes, or until they feel stiff.
11. Take them out of the oven and wait ten minutes to cool down.
12. To Slice: 12. Cut the baked sticks into 1/2-inch-wide slices across the diagonal with a sharp knife.

13. Put the biscotti slices back on the baking sheet with the cut side facing down.
14. To Bake Again: 14. Put the biscotti slices back in the oven for another 10 to 15 minutes or until they are dry and crisp.
15. Put them on a wire rack to cool down after taking them out of the oven.

Taro Root Coconut Cake:

INGREDIENTS: For the Taro Root Cake:

- 2 cups grated taro root (purple or white)
- 1 1/2 cups grated coconut
- 1 cup granulated sugar
- 1/2 cup coconut milk
- 1/4 cup melted unsalted butter
- 2 large eggs
- 1 tsp vanilla extract
- 1/2 tsp salt For the Taro Root Glaze (optional):
- 1/2 cup grated taro root (purple or white)
- 1/4 cup coconut milk
- 2 tbsp granulated sugar

Instructions: For the Taro Root Cake:

1. Warm your oven to 175°F (350°C) and grease a cake pan or baking dish.
2. Grass-cut taro root, coconut, sugar, coconut milk, melted unsalted butter, eggs, vanilla extract, and salt should all be mixed in a bowl. Mix everything well.

3. Put the taro root cake batter into the baking dish that has been oiled.
4. Putting it in the oven: 4. Bake for 40 to 45 minutes until the cake is set and the top is golden brown.
5. Take it out of the oven and let it cool down until it's even.
6. For the Taro Root Glaze (optional), grate the taro root and mix it with the coconut milk and sugar in a pot.
7. Stir the mixture while cooking over low heat until it turns into a sauce.
8. Could you wait for it to cool down?
9. To Serve: 9. If you're using it, drizzle the taro root sauce over the cake once it's fantastic.

GUAVA AND CREAM CHEESE CINNAMON ROLLS:

INGREDIENTS: For the Dough:

- 2 1/4 tsp active dry yeast
- 1/2 cup warm water
- 1/2 cup milk
- 1/4 cup granulated sugar
- 1/3 cup unsalted butter, melted
- 1 tsp salt
- 2 large eggs
- 4 cups all-purpose flour For the Filling:
- 1/2 cup guava paste, softened and diced
- 4 oz cream cheese, softened

- 1/2 cup brown sugar
- 1 1/2 tsp ground cinnamon For the Cream Cheese Glaze:
- 4 oz cream cheese, softened
- 1/4 cup unsalted butter, softened
- 1 cup powdered sugar
- 1 tsp vanilla extract

Instructions: For the Dough:

1. Mix the active dry yeast with warm water in a small bowl. Let it sit for five minutes or until it foams up.
2. Melt the unsalted butter and add it to a big bowl. Then add the eggs and mix them in.
3. Add the yeast combination and mix it in.
4. Add the all-purpose flour and mix one cup at a time until a soft dough forms.
5. Knead the dough on a lightly floured surface for 5 to 7 minutes to make it smooth and stretchy.
6. Cover the dough and set it in a buttered bowl. Let it rise in a warm place for about an hour, or until it doubles in size.
7. To make the filling: 7. Put the melted cream cheese, diced guava paste, brown sugar, and ground cinnamon in a bowl until they are well mixed.
8. To Put Together: 8. Heat the oven to 350°F (175°C) and grease a 9x13-inch baking dish.
9. Spread the dough out on a floured surface and press it down so it's about 12 inches by 18 inches.
10. Cover the dough with the guava and cream cheese sauce.
11. 11. Start rolling the dough into a log shape from the long edge clockwise.
12. The log should be cut into 12 equal pieces.
13. To bake: 13. Put the cinnamon roll slices in the baking dish that has been cleared out.

14. After the hot oven, bake the rolls for 25 to 30 minutes or until golden brown and fully cooked.
15. To make the cream cheese glaze, 15. Put the melted cream cheese, fat-free butter, powdered sugar, and vanilla extract in a bowl until the mixture is smooth and creamy.
16. To Glaze: 16. Cover the warm cinnamon rolls with the cream cheese glaze.
17. Enjoy the Guava and Cream Cheese Cinnamon Rolls while they are still warm.

COCONUT CREAM PUFFS:

INGREDIENTS: For the Cream Puffs:

- 1/2 cup unsalted butter
- 1 cup water
- 1/4 tsp salt
- 1 cup all-purpose flour
- 4 large eggs For the Coconut Cream Filling:
- 1 can (13.5 oz) coconut milk
- 1/2 cup granulated sugar
- 1/4 cup cornstarch
- 1/4 tsp salt
- 4 large egg yolks
- 2 tbsp unsalted butter
- 1 tsp coconut extract For the Coconut Glaze:
- 1 cup powdered sugar

- 2-3 tbsp coconut milk
- Shredded coconut for garnish (optional)

Instructions: For the Cream Puffs:

1. Warm the oven up to 200°C (400°F). Put parchment paper on the bottom of a baking sheet.
2. Put the unsalted butter, water, and salt in a pot. Slowly raise the heat until the mixture starts to boil.
3. Put the pan back on the stove and add the all-purpose flour. Stir the flour in until a smooth dough forms.
4. Each time you add an egg, mix the dough well afterward so it is smooth and shiny.
5. Place dough spoonfuls on the baking sheet that has been prepared, leaving room between them.
6. The cream puffs should be baked in a hot oven for 30 to 35 minutes or until they are puffed up and golden brown.
7. Now, take them out of the oven and let them cool down.
8. To fill with coconut cream: 8. Put the coconut milk, sugar, cornstarch, and salt in a pot and mix them.
9. Whisk the egg whites in a different bowl.
10. Stir the coconut milk mixture over medium-low heat until it gets thick.
11. To temper the egg whites, slowly whisk in a little hot mixture at a time.
12. Put the egg whites that have been tempered back into the saucepan with the rest of the coconut milk mixture.
13. Stir the filling as you cook until it gets thicker and gently boils.
14. Take it off the heat and mix the cream cheese and coconut flavor.
15. Wait until the coconut cream filling is cool enough to touch.

16. To Fill: 16. Ensure they are both calm Before filling the cream puffs. Then, cut them in half horizontally and fill them with the coconut cream.
17. Number of steps for the coconut glaze: 17. Whisk the powdered sugar and coconut milk together until the mixture is smooth like glaze.
18. Put the coconut glaze on top of the cream puffs that have been filled.
19. If you want, you can top it off with shredded coconut.
20. Have fun with the Coconut Cream Puffs!

CARAMELIZED GUAVA WITH WHIPPED CREAM:

INGREDIENTS:

- 2 ripe guavas, peeled, seeded, and sliced
- 1/4 cup granulated sugar
- 1/4 cup water
- 1 cup heavy cream
- 2 tbsp powdered sugar
- 1/2 tsp vanilla extract

Instructions: For the Caramelized Guava:

1. Put the water and powdered sugar in a saucepan and mix them.
2. Stir the mixture while heating it over medium-high heat until the sugar melts.

3. Cook the sliced guavas in the syrup until they get soft and the syrup gets thick and caramelized.
4. Take it off the heat and let it cool down.
5. To make the whipped cream: 5. Put heavy cream, powdered sugar, and vanilla extract in a bowl and beat them together until stiff peaks form.
6. To Give: 6. Put the guava caramelized into serving plates. Add a dollop of whipped cream on top of each dish.
7. Enjoy the guava that has been caramelized with whipped cream!

GUAVA AND CHEESE STUFFED PANCAKES:

INGREDIENTS: For the Pancake Batter:

- 1 cup all-purpose flour
- 2 tbsp granulated sugar
- 1 tsp baking powder
- 1/2 tsp baking soda
- 1/4 tsp salt
- 1 cup buttermilk
- 1 large egg
- 2 tbsp unsalted butter, melted
- 1/2 tsp vanilla extract For the Guava and Cheese Filling:
- 1/2 cup guava paste, softened and diced
- 4 oz cream cheese, softened

Instructions: For the Pancake Batter:

1. Mix the all-purpose flour, sugar, baking powder, baking soda, and salt in a bowl using a whisk to make the dough.
2. The buttermilk, egg, melted unsalted butter, and vanilla extract should all be mixed in a different bowl (with a whisk).
3. Add the wet ingredients to the dry ones and mix them just until they are mixed.
4. To fill the pie with guava and cheese: 4. Put the softened cream cheese and diced guava paste in a bowl and mix them until they are well mixed.
5. Steps to Make Stuffed Pancakes: 5. Spread oil on a pan or nonstick skillet and heat it over medium-low heat.
6. Put some pancake batter on the skillet to make a small pancake.
7. Put a small amount of the guava and cheese filling in the middle of the pancake.
8. Add a little more pancake batter on top to cover the filling.
9. Once the top starts to bubble, flip it over and cook the other side until it's golden brown and done all the way through.
10. To Give: 10. Toast the pancakes and top them with guava and cheese. Serve them warm with powdered sugar or syrup.
11. Have fun!

PINEAPPLE COCONUT TART:

INGREDIENTS: For the Tart Crust:

- 1 1/2 cups all-purpose flour
- 1/4 cup granulated sugar
- 1/4 tsp salt
- 1/2 cup unsalted butter, cold and cubed
- 1 large egg yolk
- 2 tbsp ice water For the Pineapple Coconut Filling:
- 1 can (20 oz) crushed pineapple, drained
- 1 1/2 cups shredded coconut
- 1/2 cup granulated sugar
- 2 large eggs
- 1/2 tsp vanilla extract
- 1/4 cup unsalted butter, melted
- 2 tbsp all-purpose flour
- 1/4 tsp salt

Instructions: For the Tart Crust:

1. Mix the all-purpose flour, white sugar, and salt in a bowl.
2. You can use a pastry cutter or your fingers to work the cold, cubed, unsalted butter into the flour until it looks like small crumbs.
3. Mix the egg yolk and ice water in a small bowl.
4. Mix the egg yolk mixture into the flour mixture slowly, then keep mixing until the dough comes together.
5. Put the dough in the fridge for at least 30 minutes after making a disc out of it.
6. For the filling made of pineapple and coconut: 6. Crushed pineapple that has been drained, shredded coconut, sugar, eggs, vanilla extract, melted unsalted butter, all-

purpose flour, and salt should all be put in a bowl. Mix everything well.
7. To Put It Together: 7. Heat the oven to 350°F (175°C) and grease a tart pan.
8. Roll out the cold tart dough into a circle that fits the pan on a floured surface.
9. Fit the dough into the tart pan and cut off any extra.
10. Fill the tart shell with the pineapple coconut filling.
11. 11. Put the pie in an oven that has already been heated for 40 to 45 minutes, or until the filling is set and the dough is golden brown.
12. 12. Let the Pineapple Coconut Tart cool down before you serve it.
13. Cut it up and enjoy!

CUBAN COFFEE MOUSSE CAKE:

INGREDIENTS: For the Cake:

- 1 box chocolate cake mix (and ingredients listed on the box) For the Cuban Coffee Mousse:
- 1 1/2 cups heavy cream
- 1/2 cup sweetened condensed milk
- 2 tbsp Cuban coffee (strongly brewed)
- 1 tsp vanilla extract
- 1 envelope unflavored gelatin (about 2 1/4 tsp)
- 2 tbsp water For the Chocolate Ganache:
- 1/2 cup heavy cream
- 1 cup semi-sweet chocolate chips

- 1 tbsp butter

Instructions: For the Cake:

1. Follow the directions on the box to make and bake the chocolate cake. Allow it to cool down.
2. To make the Cuban Coffee Mousse: 2. Sprinkle the gelatin over the water in a small bowl. Let it sit for a few minutes to get soft.
3. Get the heavy cream hot in a pot, but don't let it boil.
4. The cream should be taken off the heat, and the sweetened condensed milk, brewed Cuban coffee, and vanilla extract should be mixed in.
5. Mix the melted gelatin into the cream mixture and keep stirring until it's all mixed in.
6. Wait until the mixture is cool enough to touch.
7. To Put Together: 7. If you need to, use a sharp knife to level the cake after it has cooled.
8. Lay the cake out flat and cut it into two even pieces.
9. Put one piece of the cake in a dish to serve.
10. Spread half of the Cuban Coffee Mousse mix on top of the bottom layer of cake.
11. Put the second piece of cake on top, then pour the rest of the mousse over it.
12. Put the cake in the fridge for a few hours or overnight to let it set.
13. These numbers are for the chocolate ganache: 13. Get the heavy cream hot in a small pot, but don't boil it.
14. Take it off the heat and add the butter and semisweet chocolate chips. Could you wait a minute for it to melt?
15. The ganache should be smooth and shiny after being stirred.
16. Allow it to cool a bit.

17. To End: 17. Cover the mousse cake with the chocolate frosting.
18. Put the ganache back in the fridge for another hour to set.
19. Enjoy the Cuban Coffee Mousse Cake while it's still cold.

CHOCOLATE COCONUT RICE KRISPIE TREATS:

INGREDIENTS:

- 6 cups Rice Krispies cereal
- 3 cups semi-sweet chocolate chips
- 1 1/2 cups shredded coconut
- 1/2 cup unsalted butter
- 1 can (14 oz) sweetened condensed milk
- 1 tsp vanilla extract
- Pinch of salt

Instructions:

1. Put parchment paper around the edges of a 9x13-inch baking dish, leaving some overflow to make it easy to take off.
2. Mix the Rice Krispies cereal and shredded coconut in a big bowl. Put away.
3. Melt the unsalted butter and semisweet chocolate chips in a pot over low heat. Stir the mixture until it is smooth and well mixed.

4. Take the pan off the heat and add the vanilla extract, sweetened condensed milk, and a pinch of salt.
5. Put the chocolate mix on top of the coconut and Rice Krispies. Make sure it's well covered.
6. Firmly press the mixture into the baking dish that has been prepared.
7. Set: 7. Put the treats in the fridge for at least two hours or until set.
8. To Give: 8. Use the extra piece of parchment paper to lift the treats from the dish.
9. Chocolate Coconut Rice Krispie Treats should be served cut into pieces. Have fun!

MANGO AND COCONUT SCONES:

INGREDIENTS:

- 2 cups all-purpose flour
- 1/4 cup granulated sugar
- 1 tbsp baking powder
- 1/2 tsp salt
- 1/2 cup unsalted butter, cold and cubed
- 1/2 cup shredded coconut
- 1/2 cup diced mango
- 2/3 cup coconut milk
- 1 tsp vanilla extract
- 1 large egg, beaten (for egg wash)
- Additional shredded coconut for topping (optional)

Instructions:

1. Warm your oven to 400°F (200°C) and put parchment paper on a baking sheet.
2. Mix the all-purpose flour, sugar, baking powder, and salt in a bowl using a whisk.
3. Add the cold, cubed butter that doesn't have salt to the flour mix. You can use your fingers or a pastry cutter to cut the butter into the flour until the mixture resembles big crumbs.
4. Add the chopped mango and coconut flakes and mix them in.
5. Mix the vanilla extract and coconut milk in a different bowl.
6. Add the wet ingredients to the dry ones slowly while stirring them until the dough comes together.
7. To make the dough less sticky, spread it out on a floured surface and knead it a few times.
8. Make a circle out of the dough that is about an inch thick. Eight pieces should be cut out of the circle.
9. To Bake: 9. Place the scones on the baking sheet that has been prepared, leaving some room between each one.
10. Brush the scones' tops with the beaten egg; if you want, add more chopped coconut on top.
11. After the hot oven, bake the scones for 15 to 18 minutes or until golden brown and fully cooked.
12. To Give: 12. Before serving the Mango and Coconut Scones, let them cool down. Have fun!

GUAVA AND CHEESE STUFFED DONUTS:

INGREDIENTS: For the Donut Dough:

- 2 1/4 tsp active dry yeast
- 1/2 cup warm milk
- 1/4 cup granulated sugar
- 2 1/2 cups all-purpose flour
- 1/2 tsp salt
- 2 large eggs
- 1/4 cup unsalted butter, softened For the Guava and Cheese Filling:
- 1/2 cup guava paste, softened and diced
- 4 oz cream cheese, softened For Frying:
- Vegetable oil For the Glaze:
- 1 cup powdered sugar
- 2-3 tbsp milk
- 1/2 tsp vanilla extract

Instructions: For the Donut Dough:

1. Warm the milk in a small bowl and mix in the active dry yeast. Let it sit for five minutes or so until it foams up.
2. Granulated sugar, all-purpose flour, and salt should all be mixed in a big bowl.
3. The yeast mixture, eggs, and pure butter that has been melted should be added to the dry ingredients. Mix until you get a soft dough.

4. For five to seven minutes, knead the dough on a floured surface until it's smooth and springy.
5. Cover the dough and set it in a buttered bowl. Let it rise in a warm place for one to two hours, or until it goes double in size.
6. Make the filling with guava and cheese: 6. Put the softened cream cheese and diced guava paste in a bowl until they are well mixed.
7. To Put Together: 7. Pinch the dough and plop it down on a floured surface. Roll it out into a big square that's about 1/2 inch thick.
8. Cut the dough into donut forms with a round cookie cutter.
9. Put a small amount of the cheese and guava filling in the middle of half of the donut shapes.
10. Seal the top of the filled donut along the sides with another donut shape. This will make a stuffed donut.
11. Could you do it again with the rest of the dough?
12. 12. Heat vegetable oil to 350°F (175°C) in a deep pan or a pot with a heavy bottom.
13. Slowly fry the stuffed donuts one at a time until both sides are golden brown, which should take about two to three minutes per side.
14. Take the donuts out of the oil with a forked spoon and let them drain on paper towels.
15. For the Paint: 15. Mix the powdered sugar, milk, and vanilla extract in a bowl with a whisk until the glaze is smooth.
16. Cover the fried donuts with the sauce by dipping them in it.
17. To Give: 17. Enjoy the Guava and Cheese Stuffed Donuts while they are still warm.

TARO ROOT AND COCONUT TAPIOCA PUDDING:

INGREDIENTS:

- 1 cup small pearl tapioca
- 4 cups water
- 1 cup taro root, peeled and diced
- 1 can (13.5 oz) coconut milk
- 1/2 cup granulated sugar
- 1/2 tsp vanilla extract
- A pinch of salt
- Shredded coconut for garnish (optional)

Instructions:

1. Run cold water over the small pearl tapioca and let it drain.
2. Tapioca and water should be mixed in a pot. Heat it and bring it to a boil.
3. Turn down the heat and let it simmer for 15 to 20 minutes, stirring now and then, until the tapioca pearls are clear.
4. Dice the taro root and put it in a different pot. Add the coconut milk, sugar, vanilla extract, and a pinch of salt.
5. Over medium-low heat, bring the mixture to a boil and stir it often until the taro root is soft and the sauce gets a little thicker.

6. In a serving bowl, mix the cooked tapioca and taro root. Combine well.
7. To Give: 7. If you want, you can top it off with shredded coconut.
8. You can serve the Taro Root and Coconut Tapioca Pudding warm or cold. Have fun!

COCONUT ALMOND JOY BARS:

INGREDIENTS:

- 2 cups sweetened shredded coconut
- 1 can (14 oz) sweetened condensed milk
- 1 tsp vanilla extract
- 1/2 cup chopped almonds
- 1 cup semi-sweet chocolate chips
- 2 tbsp unsalted butter

Instructions:

1. Warm the oven up to 175°F (350°F). Put parchment paper around the edges of an 8x8-inch baking pan, leaving some overflow to make it easy to take off.
2. For the Shell of Coconut: 2. Mix the sweetened shredded coconut, sweetened condensed milk, and vanilla flavor in a bowl.
3. It's time to add the chopped nuts.
4. Press the coconut mixture into the baking pan that has been set up.

5. 5. Put the pan in an oven that has been hot for 20 to 25 minutes or until the edges are golden brown.
6. How to make the chocolate topping: 6. Preheat the microwave to low power and cook the unsalted butter and semisweet chocolate chips in bowl. Stir the mixture every 30 seconds until it is smooth.
7. 7. Spread the melted chocolate evenly over the baked coconut layer to finish.
8. Wait for the chocolate to set and the bars to cool down.
9. 9. Use the extra piece of parchment paper to lift the Coconut Almond Joy Bars out of the pan.
10. Serve it cut up into pieces. Have fun!

CARAMELIZED BANANA BREAD PUDDING:

INGREDIENTS:

- 4 ripe bananas, peeled and sliced
- 4 cups cubed day-old bread (such as French bread)
- 2 cups milk
- 3/4 cup granulated sugar
- 4 large eggs
- 1 tsp vanilla extract
- 1/4 tsp ground cinnamon
- A pinch of salt
- 1/4 cup unsalted butter, melted

Instructions:

1. Warm the oven up to 175°F (350°F). Prepare a 9x13-inch baking dish by greasing it.
2. For the bananas that have been caramelized: 2. Melt 2 tablespoons of butter over medium-low heat in a pan.
3. Add the banana slices and cook them until both sides are caramelized and golden brown. Take it off the heat and set it aside.
4. To make the bread pudding: 4. Mix the cubed bread and caramelized bananas in a big bowl.
5. You must mix the milk, sugar, eggs, vanilla extract, ground cinnamon, and a pinch of salt in a different bowl.
6. Cover the bananas and bread with the egg mix. Carefully press down on the bread to ensure it soaks up the water.
7. Pour the melted butter that doesn't have salt on top.
8. How to Bake: 8. Warm the oven up and put the bread pudding in it. Bake for 45 to 50 minutes or until the top is golden brown and the pudding is set.
9. To Give: 9. let the Caramelized Banana Bread Pudding cool down a bit before serving. Have fun!

GUAVA AND CREAM CHEESE BREAD:

INGREDIENTS:

- 1 loaf of French bread or Cuban bread
- 1/2 cup guava paste, softened and diced
- 4 oz cream cheese, softened
- 1/4 cup unsalted butter, melted
- 1/4 cup granulated sugar

- 1/2 tsp vanilla extract

Instructions:

1. Warm the oven up to 175°F (350°F).
2. To make the filling: 2. Put the melted cream cheese, diced guava paste, sugar, and vanilla extract in a bowl. Mix the ingredients until they are well blended.
3. To Put Together: 3. Cut the Cuban or French bread half across the grain.
4. Cut a hole in the middle of each half of the bread to make a well for the filling.
5. Fill the holes in both halves of the bread with the guava and cream cheese filling.
6. Put the two halves of bread back together to make a whole loaf.
7. To bake: 7. Put foil around the loaf that has been filled.
8. 8. Put the loaf in a hot oven for 20 to 25 minutes or until the bread is warm and the filling is soft and mushy.
9. 9. Cut the Guava and Cream Cheese Bread into pieces and serve it while it's still warm. Have fun!

CUBAN COFFEE TIRAMISU CAKE:

INGREDIENTS: For the Cake Layers:

- 1 box coffee-flavored cake mix (and ingredients listed on the box) For the Tiramisu Filling:
- 1 cup mascarpone cheese
- 1 cup heavy cream

- 1/2 cup granulated sugar
- 1 tsp vanilla extract
- 2 tbsp Cuban coffee (strongly brewed)
- 2 tbsp coffee liqueur (optional) For the Coffee Soaking Syrup:
- 1/2 cup Cuban coffee (strongly brewed)
- 2 tbsp coffee liqueur (optional) For the Topping:
- Cocoa powder for dusting
- Chocolate shavings (optional)

Instructions: For the Cake Layers:

1. Follow the directions on the box to make and bake the coffee-flavored cake. Allow it to cool down.
2. For the tiramisu filling: 2. Put the mascarpone cheese, heavy cream, sugar, vanilla extract, hot Cuban coffee, and coffee liqueur (if using) in a bowl and mix them.
3. Whip the ingredients together until stiff peaks form.
4. For the syrup that soaks coffee: 4. In a small bowl, mix the solid Cuban coffee with the coffee liqueur, if you're using it.
5. To Put Together: 5. Once the cake is cool, cut it horizontally into two or three even pieces, whichever you like best.
6. Put a piece of the cake on a platter to serve.
7. Use a lot of the coffee soaking sauce to cover the cake layer.
8. Put some of the tiramisu filling on top of the cake that has been soaked.
9. Put another layer of filling on top of the last one to finish.
10. Topping for the Cake: 10. Put cocoa powder on top of the cake and, if you want, chocolate pieces.

11. To Serve: 11. Put the Cuban Coffee Tiramisu Cake in the fridge for a few hours or overnight to let the flavors mix.
12. Cut it up and serve it cold. Have fun!

PINEAPPLE COCONUT MUFFINS:

INGREDIENTS:

- 2 cups all-purpose flour
- 1/2 cup granulated sugar
- 2 tsp baking powder
- 1/2 tsp baking soda
- 1/2 tsp salt
- 1/2 cup unsalted butter, melted and cooled
- 1 can (8 oz) crushed pineapple, drained
- 1/2 cup shredded coconut
- 1/2 cup coconut milk
- 2 large eggs
- 1 tsp vanilla extract

Instructions:

1. Warm the oven up to 190°C (375°F). You can line a muffin tin with paper cups.
2. Mix the all-purpose flour, sugar, baking powder, baking soda, and salt in a bowl using a whisk to make the dough.
3. Melted unsalted butter, crushed pineapple, shredded coconut, eggs, and vanilla extract should all be mixed in a different bowl.

4. Add the wet ingredients to the dry ones and mix them just until they are mixed. It's okay if there are lumps; mix it sparingly.
5. Fill up about two-thirds of the way to the top of each muffin cup with batter.
6. After the oven is hot, bake the muffins for 18 to 20 minutes, or until a toothpick put into the middle comes out clean.
7. Take the muffins out of the oven and let them cool for a few minutes in the pan. Then, move them to a wire rack to cool fully.
8. Enjoy the Pineapple Coconut Muffins!

MAMEY AND COCONUT PANNA COTTA:

INGREDIENTS: For the Mamey Layer:

- 2 cups ripe mamey fruit, peeled and seeded
- 1/4 cup granulated sugar
- 1/2 cup coconut milk
- 1 envelope unflavored gelatin (about 2 1/4 tsp)
- 2 tbsp water For the Coconut Layer:
- 1 can (13.5 oz) coconut milk
- 1/4 cup granulated sugar
- 1 tsp vanilla extract
- 1 envelope unflavored gelatin (about 2 1/4 tsp)
- 2 tbsp water

Instructions: For the Mamey Layer:

1. Put the peeled and seeded mamey fruit and granulated sugar in a blender. Mix until it's smooth.
2. Sprinkle the plain gelatin over the water in a small bowl. Let it sit for a few minutes to relax.
3. Low heat should be used to warm the coconut milk in a pot, but do not boil it.
4. Take the pot off the heat and add the melted gelatin. Stir it in until it's all mixed in.
5. Mix the coconut milk mixture to the chopped mamey fruit well.
6. Fill three-quarters of each serving glass or dish to the top with the mamey mixture.
7. Please put it in the fridge for an hour or until the mamey layer sets.
8. For the layer of coconut: 8. Put the coconut milk, sugar, and vanilla extract in a pot. Heat it over low heat until it's warm but not boiling.
9. Sprinkle the plain gelatin over the water in a small bowl. Let it sit for a few minutes to relax.
10. Take the pot off the heat and add the melted gelatin. Stir it in until it's all mixed in.
11. Allow the coconut milk mix to cool down a bit.
12. Carefully pour the coconut mixture over the mamey layer in the serving glasses or plates. Fill them up to two-thirds of the way to the top.
13. Please put it in the fridge for two to three hours or until both layers are set.
14. Be sure to serve the Mamey and Coconut Panna Cotta cold. Have fun!

GUAVA AND CHEESE STUFFED BISCUITS:

INGREDIENTS: For the Biscuits:

- 2 cups all-purpose flour
- 1/4 cup granulated sugar
- 1 tbsp baking powder
- 1/2 tsp salt
- 1/2 cup unsalted butter, cold and cubed
- 1/2 cup milk
- 1/2 cup guava paste, softened and diced
- 4 oz cream cheese, softened For the Glaze:
- 1/2 cup powdered sugar
- 2-3 tbsp milk

Instructions: For the Biscuits:

1. Warm the oven up to 425°F (220°C). Put parchment paper on the bottom of a baking sheet.
2. Mix the all-purpose flour, sugar, baking powder, and salt in a bowl using a whisk.
3. Add the cold, cubed butter that doesn't have salt to the dry ingredients. You can use your fingers or a pastry cutter to cut the butter into the flour until the mixture resembles big crumbs.
4. Add the milk and stir just until it's mixed in.
5. Put the dough on a floured surface and knead it a few times until it sticks together.
6. Make the dough about 1/2 inch thick.

7. Use a cookie cutter or a glass to cut the dough into rounds.
8. In the middle of each bread round, put a small amount of the softened guava paste diced and a small amount of the softened cream cheese.
9. To make a half-moon form, fold the round biscuit over the filling. To close, press the edges together.
10. Put the filled cookies on the baking sheet that has been prepped.
11. To bake: 11. Heat the oven to 350 degrees and put the biscuits in it. Bake for 12 to 15 minutes, or until they are golden brown and fully cooked.
12. To make the glaze: 12. Put the powdered sugar and enough milk in a bowl and mix them using a whisk.
13. To serve, 13. Pour the sauce over the hot Guava and Cheese Stuffed Biscuits.
14. They are best served while they are still warm. Have fun!

CHOCOLATE COCONUT BROWNIE BITES:

INGREDIENTS: For the Brownie Base:

- 1/2 cup unsalted butter
- 1 cup granulated sugar
- 2 large eggs
- 1 tsp vanilla extract
- 1/3 cup unsweetened cocoa powder

- 1/2 cup all-purpose flour
- 1/4 tsp salt For the Coconut Topping:
- 1 1/2 cups sweetened shredded coconut
- 1/2 cup sweetened condensed milk
- 1/4 cup powdered sugar
- 1/2 tsp vanilla extract For the Chocolate Drizzle (optional):
- 1/2 cup semi-sweet chocolate chips
- 1 tsp vegetable oil

Instructions: For the Brownie Base:

1. Warm the oven up to 175°F (350°F). You can grease or line a miniature muffin tin with cupcake liners ahead of time.
2. Melt the unsalted butter over low heat in a pot. Take it off the heat and let it cool down a bit.
3. To make the frosting, put the granulated sugar, eggs, and vanilla extract in a bowl and whisk them together.
4. Mix in the butter that has melted.
5. Add the all-purpose flour, salt, and unsweetened cocoa powder and sift them in. Don't mix any further than that.
6. Add enough brownie batter to each mini muffin tin hole to fill it halfway.
7. For the Coconut Dust: 7. Put the sweetened shredded coconut, sweetened condensed milk, powdered sugar, and vanilla extract in a bowl and mix them. Mix everything well.
8. Put a little of the coconut topping on top of every brownie bite.
9. To bake: 9. After the oven is hot, bake the brownies for 12 to 15 minutes, or until they are set and the coconut topping is barely golden.

10. To make the chocolate drizzle (not required): 10. In a bowl that can go in the microwave, heat the vegetable oil and semisweet chocolate chips for 30 seconds while stirring each time.
11. Pour the chocolate over the Chocolate Coconut Brownie Bites left to cool.
12. 12. Let the cookie bites cool all the way down before serving. Have fun!

COCONUT TRES LECHES FLAN:

INGREDIENTS: For the Flan Layer:

- 1 can (14 oz) sweetened condensed milk
- 1 can (12 oz) evaporated milk
- 1 can (13.5 oz) coconut milk
- 4 large eggs
- 1 tsp vanilla extract For the Caramel Layer:
- 1 cup granulated sugar
- 1/4 cup water

Instructions: For the Caramel Layer:

1. Put the water and powdered sugar in a saucepan and mix them.
2. Move the pan around a few times while cooking over medium-low heat until the sugar turns a deep golden brown. Watch out not to burn it.

3. Spread out the caramel in a 9x13-inch baking dish by stirring it around. Keep it cool and hard.
4. For the flan layer: 4. Add the evaporated milk, coconut milk, eggs, and vanilla extract to a mixing bowl. Use an electric mixer to mix the ingredients well.
5. Pour the flan mix over the caramel set in the baking dish.
6. To bake: 6. Warm the oven up to 175°F (350°F).
7. Put the baking dish inside a bigger roasting pan to make a water bath. As much hot water as it takes to cover the sides of the baking dish with the flan should go into the roasting pan.
8. Carefully move the flan from the water bath to the oven that has already been cooked.
9. For 45 to 50 minutes, or until the flan is set and a toothpick stuck in the middle comes out clean.
10. Get the flan out of the oven and let it cool until fully relaxed.
11. For Serving: 11. Put the Coconut Tres Leches Flan in the fridge for a few hours or overnight to let the flavors mix.
12. To serve, loosen the flan by running a knife around the edges of the baking dish.
13. On top of the baking dish, put a serving plate. Flip the flan onto the platter and let the caramel drizzle over the top.
14. Cut your Coconut Tres Leches Flan up and enjoy!

TARO ROOT AND COCONUT PANCAKES:

INGREDIENTS:

- 1 cup taro root, peeled and grated
- 1 cup shredded coconut
- 1 1/2 cups all-purpose flour
- 1/4 cup granulated sugar
- 1 tsp baking powder
- 1/2 tsp baking soda
- 1/4 tsp salt
- 1 cup coconut milk
- 1/2 cup water
- 2 large eggs
- 1/4 cup unsalted butter, melted and cooled
- 1 tsp vanilla extract

Instructions:

1. Put the chopped taro root and shredded coconut in a bowl and mix them.
2. Whisk the all-purpose flour, sugar, baking powder, baking soda, and salt in a different bowl.
3. Add the eggs, melted unsalted butter, vanilla extract, and coconut milk to a different bowl, and mix them using an electric mixer.
4. Add the wet ingredients to the dry ones and mix them just until they are mixed.
5. Mix the taro root and coconut slowly.
6. Heat it up in a nonstick pan or griddle over medium heat and lightly grease it with cooking spray or more melted butter.
7. Place pancakes on the grill by pouring 1/4 cup of the batter at a time.
8. Once the top starts to bubble, flip it over and cook until the other side is golden brown.

9. Please do it again with the rest of the batter.
10. Warm up the Taro Root and Coconut Pancakes before serving. Have fun!

GUAVA AND CREAM CHEESE TWISTS:

INGREDIENTS:

- 1 sheet puff pastry, thawed
- 1/2 cup guava paste, softened and diced
- 4 oz cream cheese, softened
- 1 egg, beaten (for egg wash)
- Powdered sugar for Dusting (optional)

Instructions:

1. Warm the oven up to 190°C (375°F). Put parchment paper on the bottom of a baking sheet.
2. When the puff pastry sheet is no longer frozen, unfold it on a lightly floured surface.
3. You can cut the puff pastry sheet into quarters or rectangles, whichever you like better.
4. Put the softened cream cheese and diced guava paste in a bowl and mix them until they are well mixed.
5. Add a small amount of the guava and cream cheese mix to the middle of each puff pastry piece.
6. To make a triangle, fold one corner of the square over to the other corner. To close, press the edges together.
7. Once the baking sheet is ready, put the guava and cream cheese twists on it.

8. The egg wash should be used to cover the tops of the twists.
9. To bake: 9. The twists should be baked in a hot oven for 15 to 20 minutes or until they are puffed up and golden brown.
10. To Give: 10. Add powdered sugar on top if you like.
11. Warm up the Guava and Cream Cheese Twists before serving. Have fun!

COCONUT KEY LIME PIE:

INGREDIENTS: For the Crust:

- 1 1/2 cups graham cracker crumbs
- 1/4 cup granulated sugar
- 1/2 cup unsalted butter, melted For the Filling:
- 1 can (14 oz) sweetened condensed milk
- 4 large egg yolks
- 1/2 cup key lime juice
- 1 tsp lime zest
- 1/2 cup shredded coconut For the Topping:
- 1 cup whipped cream
- Lime slices or zest for garnish (optional)

Instructions: For the Crust:

1. Warm the oven up to 175°F (350°F).

2. Put the graham cracker crumbs, sugar, and melted unsalted butter in a bowl and mix them together. Mix everything well.
3. Put the dough in a 9-inch pie dish and press it into the bottom and sides.
4. For about 10 minutes, or until the top is just barely golden, bake in an oven that has already been heated. Take it out and let it cool down.
5. To make the filling: 5. Add the egg whites, key lime juice, and lime zest to a mixing bowl and whisk them together until the mixture is smooth.
6. Add the coconut shreds and mix them in.
7. Add the filling to the graham cracker shell that has been left to cool.
8. To bake: 8. After the oven is hot, bake the dish for 15 to 20 minutes, or until the edges are set but the middle is still a little wobbly.
9. Take the pie out of the oven and let it cool down until it's no longer hot.
10. Number 10 for the topping. Spread whipped cream on top of the pie after it has cooled down.
11. You can add lime pieces or zest as a garnish if you want.
12. 12. Put the Coconut Key Lime Pie in the fridge for a few hours or until it's completely set before serving.
13. Cut it up and serve it cold. Have fun!

CARAMELIZED PLANTAIN MOUSSE:

INGREDIENTS: For the Caramelized Plantains:

- 4 ripe plantains, peeled and sliced
- 1/2 cup brown sugar
- 1/4 cup unsalted butter
- 1/4 cup water For the Mousse:
- 2 cups heavy cream
- 1/4 cup granulated sugar
- 1 tsp vanilla extract
- 2 tsp unflavored gelatin (about 1 envelope)
- 2 tbsp water

Instructions: For the Caramelized Plantains:

1. Melt the unsalted butter over medium-low heat in a pan.
2. Mix the brown sugar and water together until the sugar is gone.
3. Slice the plantains and add them to the pan. Cook them until both sides turn caramelized and golden brown.
4. Take them off the heat and let them cool down.
5. To make the mousse: 5. Sprinkle the plain gelatin over the water in a small bowl. Let it sit for a few minutes to relax.
6. Put the heavy cream and sugar in a pot and heat them over medium-low heat. Stir the sugar until it melts.
7. Take the pot off the heat and add the melted gelatin. Stir it in until it's all mixed in.
8. Add the vanilla extract and mix well.
9. Allow the cream to cool down to room temperature.
10. To Put Together: 10. Put the cooled sautéed plantains and the cream mixture into a blender. Mix until it's smooth.
11. Put the plantain mousse that has been caramelized into glasses or plates for serving.
12. Put the mousse in the fridge for a few hours or until it sets.

13. To Give: 13. Get the Caramelized Plantain Mousse cold before you serve it. Have fun!

CUBAN COFFEE ÉCLAIRS:

INGREDIENTS: For the Éclair Shells:

- 1/2 cup unsalted butter
- 1 cup water
- 1 cup all-purpose flour
- 4 large eggs For the Cuban Coffee Pastry Cream:
- 1 1/2 cups whole milk
- 1/4 cup Cuban coffee (strongly brewed)
- 4 large egg yolks
- 1/2 cup granulated sugar
- 1/4 cup cornstarch
- 1/4 tsp salt
- 1 tsp vanilla extract For the Chocolate Glaze:
- 1/2 cup semisweet chocolate chips
- 2 tbsp unsalted butter
- 1 tbsp corn syrup (optional)
- 1/4 cup heavy cream

Instructions: For the Éclair Shells:

1. Warm the oven up to 200°C (400°F). Put parchment paper on the bottom of a baking sheet.

2. Put the unsalted butter and water in a pot. Heat it up and bring it to a boil.
3. Take the pan off the heat and quickly stir in the all-purpose flour until the dough forms a ball.
4. Move the dough to a bowl for mixing and give it time to cool down.
5. One egg should be added to the dough until it is smooth and shiny.
6. Put the dough in a pastry bag that has a big round tip on it.
7. As you prepare the baking sheet, pipe the dough into éclair shapes about 3 to 4 inches long.
8. The éclair shells should be baked in a hot oven for 30 to 35 minutes or until they are puffy and golden brown.
9. Now, take them out of the oven and let them cool down.
10. The Cuban Coffee Pastry Cream needs 10 ingredients. Mix the whole milk and strong Cuban coffee in a pot. Over medium heat, warm it up, but don't boil it.
11. Whisk the egg whites, granulated sugar, cornstarch, and salt in a different bowl until everything is well mixed.
12. Whisk the hot coffee and milk mixture into the egg yolk mixture gradually.
13. Put the mixture back in the pot. Cook it over medium heat while stirring it until it gets thicker and boils.
14. Taking it off the heat, add the vanilla extract and mix it in.
15. Place the pastry cream in a bowl, cover it with plastic wrap (right on top of the cream to avoid skin forming), and let it cool to room temperature.
16. There are 16 steps for the chocolate glaze. Put the unsalted butter, corn syrup (if using), and semisweet chocolate chips in a bowl that can go in the microwave.
17. In 30-second bursts, heat in the microwave and stir until smooth and shiny.

18. Add the heavy cream and mix it in well.
19. To Put Together: 19. Carefully cut the éclair shells in half across the middle once they are excellent.
20. Put the Cuban Coffee Pastry Cream in the bottom halves.
21. Put the top halves back on.
22. Use the chocolate glaze to cover the tops of the filled éclairs.
23. Give the glaze some time to dry.
24. Enjoy the Cuban Coffee Éclairs after you serve them.

PINEAPPLE COCONUT BREAD PUDDING:

INGREDIENTS:

- 4 cups stale bread cubes
- 1 can (14 oz) crushed pineapple, drained
- 1 cup shredded coconut
- 4 large eggs
- 1 cup granulated sugar
- 2 cups milk
- 1 tsp vanilla extract
- 1/2 tsp ground cinnamon
- 1/4 tsp salt

Instructions:

1. Warm your oven up to 175°F (350°F). Spray some cooking spray on a 9x13-inch baking dish.

2. Put the old bread cubes, drained crushed pineapple, and chopped coconut in a large bowl. Once you're done mixing, spread the batter out evenly in the baking dish that has been greased.
3. Put the eggs, granulated sugar, milk, vanilla extract, ground cinnamon, and salt in a different bowl and mix them using a whisk.
4. After mixing the eggs, add the bread and pineapple mixture and make sure all the bread is covered in the egg mixture.
5. Allow the bread to soak up the juice for ten to fifteen minutes.
6. It should be baked in a hot oven for 45 to 50 minutes or until the top is golden brown and the pudding is set.
7. After taking it out of the oven, let it cool down before serving it.
8. Give the Pineapple Coconut Bread Pudding while it's still warm. Happy eating!

GUAVA AND CHEESE STUFFED CROISSANT DONUTS:

INGREDIENTS:

- 1 can (8 oz) refrigerated croissant dough
- 4 oz cream cheese, softened
- 1/2 cup guava paste, softened and diced
- Vegetable oil for frying
- Powdered sugar for Dusting

Instructions:

1. Roll out the croissant dough in the fridge on a lightly floured surface.
2. Shape the dough into squares.
3. A small amount of softened cream cheese and diced guava paste should be put on each square.
4. Roll the dough around the filling and seal the sides to make shapes like donuts.
5. Fill a deep fryer or a big, deep pan with vegetable oil. Heat it to 350°F (175°C).
6. Fry the stuffed croissant donuts slowly for about two to three minutes or until they are golden brown on all sides.
7. Take them out of the oil and let them drain on paper towels.
8. Before you serve, sprinkle with powdered sugar.
9. Donuts stuffed with guava and cheese should be served warm. Have fun!

CHOCOLATE COCONUT CHIA PUDDING:

INGREDIENTS:

- 1/4 cup chia seeds
- 1 cup coconut milk
- 2 tbsp unsweetened cocoa powder
- 2 tbsp honey or maple syrup
- 1/2 tsp vanilla extract

- Shredded coconut and chocolate chips for topping (optional)

Instructions:

1. Chia seeds and coconut milk should be mixed in a bowl.
2. Butter, honey, maple syrup, and vanilla extract should all be added. Mix things well.
3. Cover the bowl and put it in the fridge for at least two hours or overnight. Stir the mixture every so often to keep it from sticking together.
4. Stir the pudding to make it smooth and creamy before you serve it.
5. You can serve the Chocolate Coconut Chia Pudding with chocolate chips and chopped coconut on top. Have fun!

COCONUT PECAN PIE:

INGREDIENTS: For the Pie Crust:

- 1 1/4 cups all-purpose flour
- 1/2 tsp salt
- 1/2 cup unsalted butter, cold and cubed
- 3-4 tbsp ice water For the Filling:
- 1 cup granulated sugar
- 3 large eggs
- 1 cup light corn syrup
- 1/4 cup unsalted butter, melted
- 1 tsp vanilla extract

- 1 1/2 cups shredded coconut
- 1 1/2 cups pecan halves

Instructions: For the Pie Crust:

1. Put the all-purpose flour and salt in a food processor and blend them.
2. Add the unsalted, cold butter cubes and pulse the mixture until it looks like coarse bits.
3. With each beat, add one tablespoon of ice water. This will help the dough come together.
4. Spread the dough on a floured surface and make a disk with it.
5. For at least 30 minutes, put the dough in the fridge while it's wrapped in plastic.
6. Warm the oven up to 175°F (350°F).
7. Put the chilled dough on a floured surface and roll it out. Then, put the dough in a 9-inch pie dish.
8. Cut off any extra dough and seal the ends.
9. To make the filling: 9. Put the eggs and granulated sugar in a mixing bowl and whisk them together until they are well mixed.
10. Melt the unsalted butter and add it along with the vanilla extract. Combine well.
11. The pecan halves and coconut shreds should be mixed in.
12. Put the filling into the pie shell that has been cut out.
13. To bake: 13. It should be baked in a hot oven for fifty to sixty minutes or until the filling is set and the top is golden brown.
14. You can put aluminum foil over the edges of the crust if they brown too fast.
15. Take the Coconut Pecan Pie out of the oven and cool it before serving it.

16. Let it sit at room temperature. Have fun!

TRES LECHES ICE CREAM CAKE:

INGREDIENTS: For the Cake:

- 1 box white or yellow cake mix (and ingredients listed on the box)
- 1 can (14 oz) sweetened condensed milk
- 1 can (12 oz) evaporated milk
- 1 cup whole milk For the Ice Cream:
- 1.5 quarts vanilla ice cream, softened. For the Topping:
- Whipped cream
- Maraschino cherries

Instructions: For the Cake:

1. Follow the directions on the box to make and bake the white or yellow cake.
2. Leave the cake in the pan to cool down.
3. Once the cake is cool, poke holes in it all over with a fork or stick.
4. To make the milk mix: 4. Put the sweetened condensed milk, evaporated milk, and whole milk in a bowl and mix them. Combine well.
5. Spread the milk mixture over the already cooled cake and let it soak into the holes.
6. To let the cake soak up the milk mixture, cover it and put it in the fridge for at least two hours or overnight.

7. For Putting Together: 7. Once the cake has soaked up all the milk mixture, cover the whole thing with melted vanilla ice cream.
8. Put the Tres Leches Ice Cream Cake in the freezer for at least 4 hours or until the ice cream is stiff.
9. For Giving: 9. Before serving the cake, put whipped cream and maraschino cherries on top.
10. While the cake is still cold, cut it up and serve it. Have fun!

GUAVA AND CREAM CHEESE POPSICLES:

INGREDIENTS:

- 1 cup guava juice
- 1/2 cup cream cheese, softened
- 1/4 cup granulated sugar
- 1/2 cup milk
- 1/2 tsp vanilla extract

Instructions:

1. Blend the guava juice, melted cream cheese, sugar, milk, and vanilla extract in a blender.
2. Mix the ingredients until they are smooth.
3. Place the mix into popsicle molds.
4. Place a popsicle stick in each shape.
5. Put the Guava and Cream Cheese Popsicles in the freezer for at least 4 hours or until completely frozen.

6. Pop the treats out of the pans and enjoy!

MAMEY AND COCONUT CHEESECAKE BARS:

INGREDIENTS: For the Crust:

- 1 1/2 cups graham cracker crumbs
- 1/4 cup granulated sugar
- 1/2 cup unsalted butter, melted For the Cheesecake Filling:
- 16 oz cream cheese, softened
- 1 cup granulated sugar
- 3 large eggs
- 1 tsp vanilla extract
- 1 cup mamey pulp For the Coconut Topping:
- 1 cup shredded coconut
- 1/2 cup sweetened condensed milk

Instructions: For the Crust:

1. Warm the oven up to 160°C (325°F). Put parchment paper around the edges of a 9x9-inch baking dish, leaving some overflow to make it easy to take off.
2. Mix the graham cracker crumbs, sugar, and melted unsalted butter in a bowl. Mix everything well.
3. Fill the baking dish with the mixture and press it down tightly.

4. For the Cheesecake Filling: 4. Soften the cream cheese and beat it in a bowl until it is smooth.
5. Put the eggs, vanilla extract, and granulated sugar in the bowl. Mix until everything is smooth and well-mixed.
6. Spread the cream cheese mix on top of the bread in the baking dish.
7. Using a mixer, blend the mamey pulp until it is smooth.
8. Put small amounts of the mamey sauce on the cream cheese layer.
9. For the Coconut Topping: 9. Mix the sweetened condensed milk and chopped coconut in a bowl.
10. The coconut mix should be put on top of the cheesecake.
11. To bake: 11. Warm the oven up and put the cheesecake in it. Bake for 35 to 40 minutes until the center is set and the sides are golden brown.
12. Take it out of the oven and let it cool down until it's even.
13. To Chill: 13. Put the Mamey and Coconut Cheesecake Bars in the fridge for at least 4 hours or until they are frozen and set.
14. When you're ready to serve, 14. Use the extra parchment paper to lift the bars out of the baking dish.
15. Cut it into pieces and serve it cold. Have fun!

GUAVA AND CHEESE STUFFED BEIGNETS:

INGREDIENTS: For the Beignet Dough:

- 1 1/2 cups warm water (110°F/45°C)
- 1/2 cup granulated sugar
- 2 1/4 tsp active dry yeast
- 4 cups all-purpose flour
- 1/2 tsp salt
- 1/4 cup unsalted butter, softened
- Vegetable oil for frying For the Filling:
- 1/2 cup guava paste, softened and diced
- 4 oz cream cheese, softened For Dusting:
- Powdered sugar

Instructions: For the Beignet Dough:

1. Put warm water and powdered sugar in a mixing bowl. Add the yeast to the water and let it sit for five minutes or until it starts to foam.
2. Mix the yeast with the all-purpose flour, salt, and unsalted butter that has been melted. Mix until you get a dough.
3. On a greased surface, knead the dough until it gets smooth and springy.
4. Put the dough in a bowl that has been oiled. Cover it with a damp cloth and let it rise for about two hours or until it feels double its size.
5. To Fill In and Shape: The dough should be rolled out to about 1/4-inch thick on a floured surface after it has risen.
6. A square or circle about 3 to 4 inches should be cut out of the dough.
7. Each square or circle of dough should have a small amount of warm cream cheese and guava paste diced in the middle.
8. To make a half-moon form, fold the dough over the filling. To close, press the edges together.

9. To fry: 9. Heat vegetable oil to 350°F (175°C) in a deep fryer or a big fry pan.
10. Take care when you fry the stuffed beignets. It should take about two to three minutes on each side until golden brown.
11. Take them out of the oil and let them drain on paper towels.
12. To Dust: 12. Drink powdered sugar over the Guava and Cheese Stuffed Beignets before serving.
13. Warm up the beignets and serve them. Have fun!

PINEAPPLE COCONUT RICE KRISPIE TREATS:

INGREDIENTS:

- 4 cups Rice Krispies cereal
- 10 oz marshmallows
- 1/2 cup shredded coconut
- 1/2 cup dried pineapple, chopped
- 1/4 cup unsalted butter
- 1/2 cup white chocolate chips (optional)

Instructions:

1. Put the Rice Krispies cereal, shredded coconut, and chopped dried pineapple in a big bowl. Put away.
2. Melt the unsalted butter over low heat in a pot.

3. When the butter melts, add the marshmallows and stir until they are smooth and all melted.
4. Add the melted marshmallow mixture to the cereal mix and quickly stir to mix.
5. Put the mix into a 9x13-inch baking dish that has been greased.
6. You can melt the white chocolate chips in the microwave for 30 seconds while stirring them around. Spread the white chocolate that has been melted on top of the treats.
7. Let them cool and set before cutting the Pineapple Coconut Rice Krispie Treats into pieces.
8. Serve and have fun!

CARAMELIZED MANGO SORBET:

INGREDIENTS:

- 2 large ripe mangoes, peeled, pitted, and diced
- 1/2 cup granulated sugar
- 1/4 cup water
- 1 tbsp lemon juice

Instructions:

1. Put the chopped mangoes, granulated sugar, and water in a saucepan.
2. Stir the mangoes and sugar around a few times as you cook over medium-low heat until the mangoes get soft.
3. Take the pot off the heat and let it cool down a bit.
4. Put the mango mixture in a food processor or blender.

5. Blend in the lemon juice until the mixture is smooth.
6. Put the mango puree into an ice cream maker and churn it as directed by the maker's maker.
7. Put the sorbet in a jar with a lid and freeze it for a few hours or until it gets firm.
8. For the Caramelized Mango Sorbet, scoop it out and serve it. Have fun!

CUBAN COFFEE BROWNIE TRIFLE:

INGREDIENTS: For the Brownies:

- 1 box brownie mix (and ingredients listed on the box) For the Cuban Coffee Mousse:
- 1 cup heavy cream
- 1/4 cup Cuban coffee (strongly brewed)
- 1/4 cup granulated sugar
- 1 tsp vanilla extract
- 1 tsp unflavored gelatin (about 1/2 envelope)
- 1 tbsp water For Assembly:
- Whipped cream
- Chocolate shavings (optional)

Instructions: For the Brownies:

1. Follow the directions on the box to make and bake the brownies. Allow them to cool down.

2. To make the Cuban Coffee Mousse: 2. Sprinkle the plain gelatin over the water in a small bowl. Let it sit for a few minutes to relax.
3. Put the heavy cream, Cuban coffee, sugar, and vanilla extract in a saucepan. Place it over medium-low heat and stir until the sugar melts completely.
4. Take the pot off the heat and add the melted gelatin. Stir it in until it's all mixed in.
5. Allow the coffee mix to cool down to room temperature.
6. Cut the brownies into pieces after they are excellent.
7. For the Assembly: 7. Put half of the brownie squares in a dessert dish or a clear glass bowl for serving.
8. Put half of the Cuban Coffee Mousse on top of the brownie.
9. Add another layer of brownie pieces and the rest of the Cuban Coffee Mousse.
10. If you want, you can put whipped cream and chocolate bits on top of the trifle.
11. Please put it in the fridge for at least two hours before you serve it so the tastes can mix.
12. It's best to serve the Cuban Coffee Brownie Trifle cold. Have fun!

CHOCOLATE COCONUT MOCHI:

INGREDIENTS:

- 1 cup glutinous rice flour (mochiko)
- 1/4 cup unsweetened cocoa powder

- 1/2 cup granulated sugar
- 1 cup canned coconut milk
- 1/2 cup water
- Cornstarch for Dusting

Instructions:

1. Sift the unsweetened cocoa powder, powdered sugar, and glutinous rice flour in a bowl.
2. Put the canned coconut milk and water in a pot. Over medium heat, warm it up, but don't boil it.
3. Slowly add the hot coconut milk mixture to the dry ingredients while stirring until smooth.
4. Put the mixture in a bowl that can go in the microwave.
5. Put the mix in the microwave on high for one minute, then take it out and stir it. Repeat this until the mixture gets thick and stretchy, usually taking 3–4 rounds.
6. Clean an area and sprinkle it with cornstarch.
7. Roll small amounts of the mochi mix into balls while it is still warm. To keep the balls from sticking, roll each one in cornstarch.
8. You can serve the Chocolate Coconut Mochi warm or cold. Have fun!

COCONUT LIME BARS:

INGREDIENTS: For the Crust:

- 1 1/2 cups graham cracker crumbs

- 1/4 cup granulated sugar
- 1/2 cup unsalted butter, melted For the Filling:
- 4 large eggs
- 1 1/2 cups granulated sugar
- 1/2 cup all-purpose flour
- 1/4 cup shredded coconut
- 1/2 cup lime juice (about 4-5 limes)
- Zest of 2 limes
- 1/4 cup coconut milk
- Powdered sugar for Dusting (optional)

Instructions: For the Crust:

1. Warm the oven up to 175°F (350°F).
2. Mix the graham cracker crumbs, sugar, and melted unsalted butter in a bowl. Mix everything well.
3. Put the mix in the bottom of a 9x13-inch baking dish that has been oiled.
4. For about 10 minutes, or until the top is just barely golden, bake in an oven that has already been heated. Take it out and let it cool down a bit.
5. To make the filling: 5. Put the eggs and sugar into a bowl and whisk them together until they are well mixed.
6. Put in the all-purpose flour and coconut shreds. Combine well.
7. It will be smooth after adding coconut milk, lime juice, and zest.
8. Put the lime filling on top of the shell that has been baked.
9. For baking: 9. Put the pan in an oven that has already been heated and bake for 25 to 30 minutes, or until the sides are set and the middle is still wobbly.
10. Take it out of the oven and let it cool down until it's even.

11. For Dusting: 11. If you want, sprinkle powdered sugar over the Coconut Lime Bars.
12. Put the bars in the fridge for a few hours or until they are well set.
13. 13. Cut into pieces and serve cold. Have fun!

TARO ROOT AND COCONUT CUPCAKES:

INGREDIENTS: For the Cupcakes:

- 1 1/2 cups taro root, peeled and grated
- 1 1/2 cups all-purpose flour
- 1 1/2 tsp baking powder
- 1/2 tsp baking soda
- 1/4 tsp salt
- 1/2 cup unsalted butter, softened
- 1 cup granulated sugar
- 2 large eggs
- 1 tsp vanilla extract
- 1 cup canned coconut milk For the Coconut Cream Cheese Frosting:
- 8 oz cream cheese, softened
- 1/2 cup unsalted butter, softened
- 4 cups powdered sugar
- 1/4 cup canned coconut milk
- 1 tsp vanilla extract
- Shredded coconut for garnish (optional)

Instructions: For the Cupcakes:

1. Warm the oven up to 175°F (350°F). You can line a muffin tin with cupcake cups.
2. Grate the taro root and mix it with all-purpose flour, baking powder, baking soda, and salt in a bowl. After mixing well, set it away.
3. Put the melted unsalted butter and granulated sugar in a different bowl and mix them until they are light and fluffy.
4. Beat in the eggs and vanilla extract until everything is well-mixed.
5. Add the dry ingredients mixture slowly, and alternate with the canned coconut milk. Start with the dry ingredients and end with the canned coconut milk. Mix the mix well until it's smooth.
6. The filling should be about two-thirds of the way up each cupcake liner.
7. After the oven is hot, bake the cupcakes for 18 to 20 minutes or until a toothpick stuck in the middle comes out clean.
8. Let the cupcakes cool down after taking them out of the oven before filling them.
9. For the frosting made with cream cheese and coconut: 9. Softened cream cheese and plain butter should be mixed in a bowl until they are smooth and creamy.
10. Add the powdered sugar, canned coconut milk, and vanilla extract one cup at a time. Mix the frosting well until it's fluffy and smooth.
11. For the frosting: 11. Use the Coconut Cream Cheese Frosting to decorate the cupcakes once they are completely cool.
12. If you want, you can top it off with shredded coconut.
13. Enjoy the Taro Root and Coconut Cupcakes!

GUAVA AND CREAM CHEESE FRENCH TOAST CASSEROLE:

INGREDIENTS: For the Casserole:

- 1 loaf French bread, cut into cubes
- 8 oz cream cheese, softened
- 1/2 cup guava paste, softened and diced
- 8 large eggs
- 2 cups whole milk
- 1/2 cup granulated sugar
- 1 tsp vanilla extract For the Topping:
- 1/2 cup granulated sugar
- 1/2 cup all-purpose flour
- 1/2 cup unsalted butter, cold and cubed
- Powdered sugar for Dusting

Instructions: For the Casserole:

1. Prepare a 9x13-inch baking dish by greasing it.
2. In the baking dish, put half of the French bread cubes.
3. Spread the melted cream cheese and diced guava paste on the bread with spoonfuls.
4. Add the last few French bread cubes on top.
5. Whisk the eggs, whole milk, sugar, and vanilla extract together until everything is well-mixed.
6. Ensure the bread cubes are covered in the egg mixture as you pour it over them.

7. This will help the flavors mix. Put the baking dish in the fridge for at least two hours or overnight.
8. For the Top: 8. Mix the all-purpose flour and powdered sugar in a bowl.
9. Add the cold, cubed raw butter and mix it in until it looks like big crumbs.
10. To bake: 10. Warm the oven up to 175°F (350°F).
11. Spread the topping mixture out over the dish in a thin layer.
12. Warm the oven up and put the dish in it. Bake for 45 to 55 minutes until the top is golden brown and the casserole is set.
13. Take it out of the oven and let it cool down a bit.
14. For sweeping: 14. Before you serve the Guava and Cream Cheese French Toast Casserole, sprinkle it with powdered sugar.
15. Enjoy while still warm!

GUAVA AND CHEESE ICE CREAM:

INGREDIENTS:

- 2 cups heavy cream
- 1 cup whole milk
- 3/4 cup granulated sugar
- 4 oz cream cheese, softened
- 1/2 cup guava paste, softened and diced

Instructions:

1. Whisk the heavy cream, whole milk, and sugar together until the sugar is thoroughly mixed.
2. Cream cheese should be melted. In a different bowl, beat it until it's smooth.
3. Slowly add the cream mixture to the softened cream cheese while mixing the whole thing.
4. Put the liquid into an ice cream maker and churn it as directed by the maker's maker.
5. Wait to stir the ice cream until the diced guava paste is added.
6. Move the Guava and Cheese Ice Cream to a container with a lid. Freeze it for a few hours or until it's solid.
7. Serve the ice cream with a scoop. Have fun!

PINEAPPLE COCONUT CHOCOLATE FONDUE:

INGREDIENTS:

- 1 cup canned coconut milk
- 1 cup semisweet chocolate chips
- 1 cup crushed pineapple, drained
- Assorted dippers (e.g., marshmallows, strawberries, banana slices, pretzels)

Instructions:

1. Bring the canned coconut milk to a simmer over medium-low heat in a pot. Do not let it boil.

2. When the coconut milk is hot, add the semisweet chocolate chips.
3. Keep stirring the mixture until all the chocolate is melted and smooth.
4. Take it off the heat and add the crushed, drained pineapple.
5. Put the Pineapple Coconut Chocolate Fondue in a fondue pot or a serving dish that can handle the heat.
6. Serve with a variety of crackers to dip into the fondue. Have fun!

MAMEY AND COCONUT TRES LECHES CAKE:

INGREDIENTS: For the Cake:

- 1 cup all-purpose flour
- 1 1/2 tsp baking powder
- 1/4 tsp salt
- 4 large eggs
- 1 cup granulated sugar
- 1/4 cup whole milk
- 1 tsp vanilla extract
- 1 cup mamey pulp For the Tres Leches Mixture:
- 1 can (14 oz) sweetened condensed milk
- 1 can (12 oz) evaporated milk
- 1/2 cup canned coconut milk For the Whipped Cream Topping:

- 1 cup heavy cream
- 2 tbsp powdered sugar
- 1 tsp vanilla extract
- Mamey slices and shredded coconut for garnish (optional)

Instructions: For the Cake:

1. Warm the oven up to 175°F (350°F). A 9x13-inch baking dish should be greased and floured.
2. Whisk the all-purpose flour, baking powder, and salt in a bowl. Put away.
3. Beat the eggs and sugar until they are light and fluffy in a different bowl.
4. Mix the eggs and vanilla flavor. Then add the whole milk. Combine well.
5. Add the dry and wet ingredients one at a time, stirring well after each addition.
6. Add the mamey mush and mix it in.
7. Pour the batter into the baking dish that has been set up.
8. For the mix of Tres Leches: 8. In a different bowl, mix the evaporated milk, sweetened condensed milk, and canned coconut milk with a whisk.
9. Spread the Tres Leches mixture out over the cake that has been baked.
10. Allow the cake to sit for around 30 minutes so that the juice can soak in.
11. On top of the whipped cream: 11. Put the heavy cream, powdered sugar, and vanilla extract in a bowl and beat them together until stiff peaks form.
12. Cover the cake with the whipped cream.
13. 13. you can decorate the Mamey and Coconut Tres Leches Cake with coconut shreds and mamey pieces.

14. Please put it in the fridge for a few hours or until it's freezing.
15. Cut and serve. Have fun!

GUAVA AND CHEESE STUFFED CINNAMON SUGAR PRETZELS:

INGREDIENTS: For the Pretzel Dough:

- 1 1/2 cups warm water (110°F/45°C)
- 1 packet (2 1/4 tsp) active dry yeast
- 1 tsp salt
- 1 tbsp granulated sugar
- 4 cups all-purpose flour
- 1/4 cup unsalted butter, melted For the Filling:
- 1/2 cup guava paste, softened and diced
- 4 oz cream cheese, softened For Boiling:
- 10 cups water
- 2/3 cup baking soda For Topping:
- 1/4 cup granulated sugar
- 1 tsp ground cinnamon
- 2 tbsp unsalted butter, melted

Instructions: For the Pretzel Dough:

1. Warm the water and add the active dry yeast, salt, and granulated sugar to a bowl. Leave it alone for five minutes or until it foams up.

2. Add the all-purpose flour and melted unsalted butter to the yeast mixture gradually. Mix until a dough starts to form.
3. On a greased surface, knead the dough until it gets smooth and springy.
4. Put the dough in a bowl that has been oiled. Cover it with a damp cloth and let it rise for an hour or until it has doubled.
5. For shape and filling: 5. The dough has risen, so punch it down and split it into 12 equal pieces.
6. Make a long rope out of each piece, about 18 inches long.
7. Make each rope a little flatter and put a small amount of melted cream cheese and diced guava paste in the middle of each one.
8. To make a pretzel, fold the dough over the filling. To close, press the edges together.
9. To boil: 9. Warm the oven to 230°C (450°F). Put parchment paper on the bottom of a baking sheet.
10. Bring 10 cups of water and baking soda to a boil in a big pot.
11. Carefully put one pretzel at a time into the boiling water for 30 seconds. Using a slotted spoon, take each one out and place it on the baking sheet that has been prepped.
12. 12. Mix the granulated sugar and ground cinnamon in a dish.
13. Spread some hot unsalted butter on each pretzel, then cover them with the cinnamon sugar mix.
14. To bake: 14. The pretzels should be baked in a hot oven for 10 to 12 minutes or until golden brown.
15. Take them out of the oven and let them cool down before serving them.
16. Warm up the Cinnamon Sugar Pretzels Stuffed with Guava and Cheese and serve them. Have fun!

COCONUT ALMOND JOY BARS:

INGREDIENTS:

- 1 1/2 cups sweetened shredded coconut
- 1 cup sweetened condensed milk
- 1 tsp vanilla extract
- 1 1/2 cups semisweet chocolate chips
- 1/2 cup almonds, chopped
- 1/4 cup unsalted butter, melted

Instructions:

1. Warm the oven up to 175°F (350°F). Put parchment paper around the edges of an 8x8-inch baking pan, leaving some overflow to make it easy to take off.
2. Mix the sweetened shredded coconut, sweetened condensed milk, and vanilla extract in a bowl. Combine well.
3. Spread the mixture out evenly in the baking pan that has been prepared.
4. In a bowl that can go in the microwave, heat the unsalted butter and semisweet chocolate chips for 30 seconds at a time, stirring each time until the mixture is smooth.
5. The chocolate mixture should be poured over the coconut layer in the baking pan.
6. The chopped nuts should be put on top of the chocolate layer.
7. After the oven is hot, bake for 25 to 30 minutes or until the edges are golden brown.

8. After taking the bars out of the oven, let them cool in the pan.
9. After the bars have cooled, lift the extra parchment paper out of the pan.
10. Enjoy! Cut it into pieces.

CARAMELIZED BANANA SPLIT:

INGREDIENTS:

- 2 ripe bananas, halved lengthwise
- 1/4 cup granulated sugar
- 2 tbsp unsalted butter
- Vanilla ice cream
- Whipped cream
- Chocolate syrup
- Chopped nuts (e.g., peanuts or walnuts)
- Maraschino cherries

Instructions:

1. Melt the unsalted butter over medium-low heat in a pan.
2. Spread the powdered sugar over the hot butter in a thin layer.
3. Put the banana halves in the pan with the cut side down.
4. The bananas should be cooked on each side for two to three minutes or until they turn golden brown and toasted.
5. Take the browned banana halves out of the pan.

6. Put a scoop of vanilla ice cream in a bowl or serving dish. This is the first step in making the Caramelized Banana Split.
7. Put the toasted banana halves on top of the ice cream.
8. Pour chocolate sauce over the top, top with whipped cream, add chopped nuts, and finish with maraschino cherries.
9. Enjoy the Caramelized Banana Split after you've made it.

CUBAN COFFEE TRES LECHES FLAN:

INGREDIENTS: For the Flan Layer:

- 1 cup granulated sugar
- 2 tbsp water
- 4 large eggs
- 1 can (14 oz) sweetened condensed milk
- 1 can (12 oz) evaporated milk
- 1/2 cup brewed Cuban coffee, cooled
- 1 tsp vanilla extract For the Tres Leches Layer:
- 1 can (14 oz) sweetened condensed milk
- 1 can (12 oz) evaporated milk
- 1/2 cup whole milk

Instructions: For the Flan Layer:

1. Warm the oven up to 175°F (350°F).

2. Put the water and powdered sugar in a saucepan and mix them. Please put it on medium-high heat, and don't stir it until it turns brown and turns into caramel.
3. Place the caramel in the bottom of a 9x13-inch baking dish and tilt it to cover the whole bottom. Let it cool down and get hard.
4. Whisk the eggs, sweetened condensed milk, evaporated milk, hot Cuban coffee, and vanilla extract until everything is well mixed.
5. Pour the flan mix over the caramel set in the baking dish.
6. To get to the Tres Leches Layer: 6. In a different bowl, mix the whole milk, evaporated milk, and sweetened condensed milk with a whisk.
7. With care, pour the Tres Leches mixture on top of the flan layer in the baking dish.
8. To bake: 8. Throw metal foil over the baking dish to protect it.
9. Put the baking dish with the lid into a bigger roasting pan. Put hot water in the roasting pan until it comes halfway up the sides of the baking dish.
10. After the oven is hot, bake the flan for 50 to 60 minutes or until it is set and a knife stuck in it comes out clean.
11. Once the dish is cool enough to touch, take it out of the water bath.
12. Please put it in the fridge for at least 4 hours or until it's freezing.
13. To Give: 13. Run a knife carefully around the edges of the baking dish to loosen the flan before serving.
14. Turn the Cuban Coffee Tres Leches Flan onto a serving dish so the caramel can drip on top.
15. Cut it up and serve it cold. Have fun with your decadent treat!

TARO ROOT AND COCONUT POPSICLES:

INGREDIENTS:

- 1 cup cooked and mashed taro root
- 1/2 cup canned coconut milk
- 1/4 cup sweetened condensed milk
- 1/4 cup granulated sugar
- 1/2 tsp vanilla extract
- Popsicle molds and sticks

Instructions:

1. Put the mashed taro root, canned coconut milk, sweetened condensed milk, sugar, and vanilla extract in a blender. Mix until it's smooth.
2. Fill popsicle molds with the taro and coconut mix.
3. Place a popsicle stick in each shape.
4. Put the popsicles in the freezer for at least 4 hours or until firm.
5. On a hot day, take these Taro Root and Coconut Popsicles out of the mold and eat them!

GUAVA AND CHEESE STUFFED MONKEY BREAD:

INGREDIENTS: For the Dough:

- 4 cups all-purpose flour
- 1/3 cup granulated sugar
- 2 1/4 tsp active dry yeast (1 packet)
- 1/2 tsp salt
- 1/2 cup unsalted butter, melted
- 1 cup warm milk
- 2 large eggs For Filling:
- 1 cup guava paste, diced
- 1 cup cream cheese, diced For Coating:
- 1/2 cup unsalted butter, melted
- 1 cup granulated sugar
- 1 tbsp ground cinnamon

Instructions: For the Dough:

1. Mix the all-purpose flour, sugar, yeast, and salt in a bowl
2. Mix the unsalted butter with the warm milk and eggs in a different bowl.
3. Slowly add the wet ingredients to the dry ones while mixing them. Do this until a dough forms.
4. Knead the dough on a greased surface to make it smooth and stretchy.
5. Put the dough in a bowl that has been oiled. Cover it with a damp cloth and let it rise for an hour or until it has doubled.
6. For the Assembly: 6. Warm the oven up to 175°F (350°F). Put some butter in a bundt pan.

7. Cut the dough into small pieces about an inch across after it has risen.
8. Spread each piece and put a small cube of cream cheese and guava paste in the middle.
9. When you fold the dough around the filling, it makes a good seal.
10. Put the cinnamon powder and powdered sugar in a bowl and mix them.
11. First, dip each filled dough ball in hot, unsalted butter. Then, roll it in the cinnamon-sugar mix.
12. Spread the dough balls out in the bundt pan that has been oiled.
13. To bake: 13. After the oven is hot, bake the monkey bread for 30 to 35 minutes or until it is golden brown and fully cooked.
14. Please remove it from the oven and let it cool for a few minutes before flipping it onto a serving plate.
15. Enjoy the warm Guava and Cheese Stuffed Monkey Bread by pulling it apart.

PINEAPPLE COCONUT CREPE CAKE:

INGREDIENTS: For the Crepes:

- 1 cup all-purpose flour
- 2 cups canned coconut milk
- 2 large eggs
- 2 tbsp granulated sugar
- 1/4 cup unsalted butter, melted

- Pinch of salt
- Butter or oil for cooking For the Filling:
- 2 cups canned crushed pineapple, drained
- 2 cups sweetened shredded coconut
- 1 1/2 cups whipped cream
- Additional shredded coconut for garnish

Instructions: For the Crepes:

1. Put the all-purpose flour, eggs, granulated sugar, melted unsalted butter, and a pinch of salt in a blender. Blend until smooth. Use a blender to make the batter smooth.
2. Put a nonstick pan on medium heat and use butter or oil to lightly coat it.
3. Add a little crepe batter to the pan and swirl it to cover the bottom evenly.
4. The crepe should be cooked on each side for one to two minutes until it turns a light brown color. Please do it again with the rest of the batter, and stack the cooked crepes on a plate.
5. To make the filling: 5. Put the shredded coconut that has been sweetened and the crushed pineapple that has been drained into a mixing bowl.
6. Add whipped cream to the crepe after putting it on a plate.
7. Put some pineapple and coconut mixture on top and spread it evenly.
8. Stack more crepes and fill them with more filling until you've used all of them.
9. Add a dollop of whipped cream on top and extra chopped coconut on top to decorate.
10. Put the Pineapple Coconut Crepe Cake in the fridge for at least two hours before you serve it. Cut it up, and enjoy!

COCONUT TAPIOCA PEARLS:

INGREDIENTS:

- 1 cup tapioca pearls
- 4 cups water
- 1 can (13.5 oz) coconut milk
- 1/2 cup granulated sugar
- Pinch of salt
- Fresh fruit (e.g., mango or lychee) for garnish (optional)

Instructions:

1. Soak the pearls in cold water until the water runs clear.
2. Bring 4 cups of water to a boil in a big pot.
3. Rinse the tapioca pearls and add them to the hot water. Stir the water slowly.
4. Turn the heat to medium, and stir the pearls now and then for 20 to 25 minutes.
5. Take the pot off the heat and let it sit for another 15 minutes so the pearls can finish cooking and soak up any extra water.
6. After cooking the tapioca pearls, drain them and rinse them under cold water to remove any extra starch.
7. Add the granulated sugar, a pinch of salt, and coconut milk to a different pot. Stir the mixture on medium heat until the sugar is gone.
8. Take the coconut milk mix off the heat and let it cool to room temperature.

9. Mix the cooked tapioca pearls with the coconut milk mixture that has been sweetened.
10. You can serve the Coconut Tapioca Pearls warm or cold; if you want, you can top them with fresh fruit.

TRES LECHES BREAD PUDDING:

INGREDIENTS:

- 6 cups cubed bread (e.g., French bread)
- 1 can (14 oz) sweetened condensed milk
- 1 can (12 oz) evaporated milk
- 1/2 cup canned coconut milk
- 4 large eggs
- 1 tsp vanilla extract
- Pinch of salt

Instructions:

1. Warm the oven up to 175°F (350°F).
2. Put the bread cubes in a 9x13-inch baking dish that has been oiled.
3. Add the evaporated milk, canned coconut milk, large eggs, vanilla extract, and a pinch of salt to a mixing bowl. Use a whisk to mix the ingredients.
4. Pour the milk mix over the bread cubes in the baking dish.
5. Soak the bread in the milk mixture for 15 to 20 minutes, pressing it down every so often to ensure it soaks up the liquid.

6. It should be baked in a hot oven for 45 to 50 minutes or until the top is golden brown and the pudding is set.
7. Take it out of the oven and let it cool down.
8. Take a bite of the warm Tres Leches Bread Pudding and enjoy it!

GUAVA AND CREAM CHEESE DANISHES:

INGREDIENTS:

- 1 sheet of puff pastry, thawed
- 4 oz cream cheese, softened
- 1/2 cup guava paste, softened and diced
- 1/4 cup granulated sugar
- 1 egg, beaten
- Powdered sugar for dusting (optional)

Instructions:

1. Warm the oven up to 200°C (400°F).
2. First, let the puff pastry sheet thaw. Then, roll it out on a lightly floured surface.
3. Cut the puff pastry into squares or shapes depending on what you like.
4. Put the melted cream cheese, diced guava paste, and granulated sugar in a mixing bowl. Mix everything well.
5. Put a small amount of the guava and cream cheese mix in the middle of each puff pastry piece.

6. Fold the puff pastry over the center to make a triangle or rectangle.
7. Seal the danishes by crimping the sides with a fork.
8. Brush the danishes with the egg wash to make the tops glossy.
9. Put the danishes on a baking sheet that has parchment paper on it.
10. The danishes should be baked in a hot oven for 15 to 20 minutes or until they are puffed up and golden brown.
11. Take them out of the oven and let them cool down a bit.
12. Add powdered sugar on top if you like.
13. If you want, you can serve the Guava and Cream Cheese Danishes warm. Have fun!

MAMEY AND COCONUT MOUSSE:

INGREDIENTS:

- 2 cups mamey pulp
- 1 can (13.5 oz) coconut milk
- 1/2 cup powdered sugar
- 1 tsp vanilla extract
- 1/4 cup heavy cream
- Fresh mamey slices or shredded coconut for garnish (optional)

Instructions:

1. Put the mamey pulp, coconut milk, powdered sugar, and vanilla extract in a mixer. Mix until it's smooth.

2. Whip the heavy cream in a different bowl until stiff peaks form.
3. Mix the coconut and mamey mixture into the whipped cream until everything is well mixed.
4. Use cups or bowls to serve the Mamey and Coconut Mousse.
5. Please put it in the fridge for at least two hours or until it's cold and set.
6. You can add fresh mamey pieces or shredded coconut as a garnish if you want.
7. Serve the mousse and enjoy the taste of the tropics!

CUBAN COFFEE MACARONS:

INGREDIENTS: For the Macarons:

- 1 3/4 cups powdered sugar
- 1 cup almond flour
- 3 large egg whites, room temperature
- 1/4 cup granulated sugar
- 1 tsp instant Cuban coffee
- Pinch of salt For the Filling:
- 4 oz cream cheese, softened
- 1/4 cup unsalted butter, softened
- 1 cup powdered sugar
- 1 tsp instant Cuban coffee
- 1 tsp vanilla extract

Instructions: For the Macarons:

1. Warm the oven up to 150°C/300°F. Put parchment paper on two baking sheets.
2. Powdered sugar and almond flour should be mixed in a food processor. Mix until everything is well mixed.
3. Put the egg whites, sugar, instant Cuban coffee, and a pinch of salt in a bowl and beat them together until stiff peaks form.
4. Mix the almond flour and sugar mixture into the egg white mixture slowly until the batter is smooth and has a ribbon texture.
5. Put the macaron batter into a bag with a round piping tip.
6. Put small rounds of batter on the baking sheets that have been prepared, leaving room between each one.
7. Tap the baking sheets on the table to get rid of any air bubbles. Then, let the macarons rest for about 30 minutes or until a skin forms on top.
8. The macarons should be baked in a hot oven for 15 to 18 minutes or until they are set and have feet.
9. Take them off the baking sheets and let them cool down.
10. To make the filling: 10. Put the softened cream cheese and butter in a bowl and mix them until they are smooth.
11. Cocoa powder, instant Cuban coffee, and vanilla extract should all be added. Mix everything by beating it.
12. To Put Together: 12. Put the shells of the macarons in order by size.
13. Spread or pipe a little of the filling on the flat side of one shell. Then, put another shell between them and join them together.
14. Please do it again with the rest of the cookies.
15. Please put it in the fridge for at least 24 hours to let the flavors mix.

16. Feel free to serve the Cuban Coffee Macarons and enjoy the delicious coffee taste.

CHOCOLATE COCONUT CREPES:

INGREDIENTS: For the Crepes:

- 1 cup all-purpose flour
- 2 large eggs
- 1 1/4 cups canned coconut milk
- 1/4 cup unsweetened cocoa powder
- 2 tbsp granulated sugar
- 2 tbsp unsalted butter, melted
- Pinch of salt For the Filling:
- 1 cup sweetened shredded coconut
- 1 cup semisweet chocolate chips
- Whipped cream (optional)
- Chocolate sauce (optional)
- Toasted coconut flakes for garnish (optional)

Instructions: For the Crepes:

1. Put the whole-wheat flour, large eggs, canned coconut milk, unsweetened cocoa powder, sugar, melted unsalted butter, and a pinch of salt in a mixer. Use a blender to make the batter smooth.
2. Put a nonstick pan on medium heat and use butter or oil to lightly coat it.

3. Add a little crepe batter to the pan and swirl it to cover the bottom evenly.
4. For about one to two minutes on each side, or until it's done, cook the crepe. Please do it again with the rest of the batter, and stack the cooked crepes on a plate.
5. To make the filling 5, mix the sweetened chopped coconut and semisweet chocolate chips in a bowl.
6. Spread a crepe on a plate and top it with some chocolate and coconut mixture.
7. Fold or roll the crepe, and do the same thing with the rest of the crepes.
8. Put whipped cream on top of the Chocolate Coconut Crepes and, if you want, drizzle them with chocolate sauce.
9. To add more taste and texture, sprinkle toasted coconut flakes on top.
10. Enjoy the chocolate and coconut pancakes after you serve them.

COCONUT BANANA BREAD PUDDING:

INGREDIENTS:

- 6 cups cubed banana bread
- 1 can (14 oz) sweetened condensed milk
- 1 can (12 oz) evaporated milk
- 1/2 cup canned coconut milk
- 4 large eggs
- 1 tsp vanilla extract

- Pinch of salt

Instructions:

1. Warm the oven up to 175°F (350°F).
2. Put the banana bread cubes in a 9x13-inch baking dish that has been oiled.
3. Add the evaporated milk, canned coconut milk, large eggs, vanilla extract, and a pinch of salt to a mixing bowl. Use a whisk to mix the ingredients.
4. Put the banana bread cubes in a baking dish and pour the milk.
5. Soak the bread in the milk mixture for 15 to 20 minutes, pressing it down every so often to ensure it soaks up the liquid.
6. It should be baked in a hot oven for 45 to 50 minutes or until the top is golden brown and the pudding is set.
7. Take it out of the oven and let it cool down for a while.
8. Enjoy the warm Coconut Banana Bread Pudding!

CARAMELIZED PLANTAIN ICE CREAM:

INGREDIENTS:

- 4 ripe plantains, peeled and sliced
- 1/2 cup granulated sugar
- 2 tbsp unsalted butter
- 1 tsp ground cinnamon

- 1 tsp vanilla extract
- 2 cups vanilla ice cream

Instructions:

1. Melt the unsalted butter over medium-low heat in a pan.
2. Place the chopped plantains on top and cover them with sugar.
3. For 5 to 7 minutes, turn the plantains over a few times to make them toasted and golden brown.
4. Add the vanilla extract and ground cinnamon, and cook for one more minute.
5. After cooking the plantains, take them off the heat and let them cool.
6. Put scoops of vanilla ice cream into bowls or plates for serving.
7. Put the plantains that have been cooked on top of the ice cream.
8. Caramelized Plantain Ice Cream should be served right away so you can enjoy the sweet and tropical tastes!

GUAVA AND CHEESE STUFFED WAFFLE CONES:

INGREDIENTS: For the Waffle Cones:

- 1 cup all-purpose flour
- 1/2 cup granulated sugar
- 1/4 cup unsalted butter, melted

- 2 large eggs
- 1 tsp vanilla extract
- Pinch of salt
- 1/2 cup whole milk For the Filling:
- Guava paste, diced
- Cream cheese, diced

Instructions: For the Waffle Cones:

1. Add the all-purpose flour, sugar, melted unsalted butter, large eggs, vanilla extract, and a pinch of salt to a mixing bowl. Use a whisk to mix the ingredients.
2. While mixing, add the whole milk until the batter is smooth.
3. Follow the directions with the waffle cone maker to heat it
4. Pour a small amount of batter in the middle of the waffle cone maker.
5. Follow the maker's instructions and close the lid. Cook the waffle cone until it is golden brown and easy to roll.
6. Take the waffle cone out of the oven and make it into a cone while it's still warm. Could you keep it in place until it hardens?
7. For the Assembly: 7. Put cream cheese and diced guava paste inside each waffle cone after it has cooled but is still soft.
8. Give your guests the Guava and Cheese Stuffed Waffle Cones and let them enjoy the sweet and creamy filling inside the crunchy cones.

PINEAPPLE COCONUT WHOOPIE PIES:

INGREDIENTS: For the Whoopie Pies:

- 2 cups all-purpose flour
- 1 tsp baking powder
- 1/2 tsp baking soda
- 1/2 tsp salt
- 1/2 cup unsalted butter, softened
- 1/2 cup granulated sugar
- 1/2 cup canned crushed pineapple, drained
- 1/4 cup canned coconut milk
- 2 large eggs
- 1 tsp vanilla extract For the Filling:
- 1/2 cup unsalted butter, softened
- 2 cups powdered sugar
- 1/4 cup canned coconut milk
- 1/2 tsp vanilla extract

Instructions: For the Whoopie Pies:

1. Warm the oven up to 175°F (350°F). Put parchment paper on baking sheets.
2. Put the all-purpose flour, baking powder, baking soda, and salt in a bowl and mix them with a whisk.
3. Put the melted unsalted butter and granulated sugar in a different bowl and mix them until they are light and fluffy.

4. Mix the crushed pineapple drained with the coconut milk from the can, the giant eggs, and the vanilla extract. Mix everything well.
5. Mix the dry ingredients into the wet ingredients one at a time until the batter is smooth.
6. Place spoonfuls of the batter on the baking sheets that have been prepared, leaving room between each one.
7. After the oven is hot, bake the whoopie pies for 10 to 12 minutes or until they are set and slightly brown.
8. Take them out of the oven and let them cool for a few minutes on the baking sheets. Then, move them to a wire rack to cool down.
9. To make the filling: 9. Put the softened unsalted butter in a bowl and beat it until it's smooth.
10. Add the powdered sugar, canned coconut milk, and vanilla extract one cup at a time. Mix the filling well until it's smooth and creamy.
11. 11. Spread a lot of the coconut filling on the flat side of one whoopie pie to put it together.
12. To make a sandwich, put another whoopie pie on top.
13. Please do it again with the rest of the filling and whoopie pies.
14. Have fun with the Pineapple Coconut Whoopie Pies!

TARO ROOT AND COCONUT BROWNIES:

INGREDIENTS:

- 1 cup taro root, cooked and mashed
- 1/2 cup canned coconut milk
- 1/2 cup unsalted butter, melted
- 1 cup granulated sugar
- 2 large eggs
- 1 tsp vanilla extract
- 1/2 cup all-purpose flour
- 1/4 cup unsweetened cocoa powder
- 1/2 tsp baking powder
- Pinch of salt

Instructions:

1. Warm the oven up to 175°F (350°F). An 8x8-inch baking pan should be greased.
2. Put the cooked and mashed taro root, canned coconut milk, melted unsalted butter, and sugar in a mixing bowl. Mix everything well.
3. Add the giant eggs and vanilla extract to the taro and coconut mix. Mix until it's smooth.
4. All-purpose flour, unsweetened cocoa powder, baking powder, and a pinch of salt should all be mixed in a different bowl using a whisk.
5. Slowly add the dry ingredients to the wet ones while stirring them together.
6. As soon as you grease the baking pan, pour the cookie batter into it.
7. In a hot oven, bake for 25 to 30 minutes or until a toothpick stuck in the middle comes out with a few moist bits on it.
8. After taking the brownies out of the oven, let them cool in the pan for a few minutes before moving them to a wire rack to cool all the way through.

9. Serve the Taro Root and Coconut Brownies by cutting them into pieces. Enjoy the unusual mix of flavors!

GUAVA AND CREAM CHEESE STUFFED CHOCOLATE TRUFFLES:

INGREDIENTS:

- 8 oz dark chocolate, chopped
- 4 oz cream cheese, softened
- 1/4 cup guava paste, diced
- Cocoa powder for dusting

Instructions:

1. Melt the dark chocolate in a bowl that can go in the microwave for 20 to 30 seconds, stirring until it's smooth and melted.
2. In a different bowl, beat the softened cream cheese until smooth.
3. Mix the cream cheese and diced guava paste together until everything is well-mixed.
4. Combine the guava and cream cheese, then mix them into the melted dark chocolate until smooth.
5. This should be put in the fridge for about an hour or until it's hard enough to handle.
6. To make truffles, take small amounts of the mixture and roll them into balls after it has been chilled.
7. Cover all of the truffles with cocoa powder by rolling them in it.

8. Fill small paper bags with the Guava and Cream Cheese Stuffed Chocolate Truffles.
9. Serve and enjoy these delicious cookies that you made yourself!

COCONUT MANGO RICE PUDDING:

INGREDIENTS:

- 1 cup jasmine rice
- 1 can (13.5 oz) coconut milk
- 1 can (14 oz) sweetened condensed milk
- 2 cups diced ripe mango
- 1/2 cup shredded coconut
- 1 tsp vanilla extract

Instructions:

1. Follow the directions on the package to cook the jasmine rice.
2. Cooked rice, coconut milk, sweetened condensed milk, diced ripe mango, shredded coconut, and vanilla extract should all be put in a pot.
3. Stir the mixture often while heating it over medium-low heat until it thickens to the desired consistency (about 15 to 20 minutes).
4. The Coconut Mango Rice Pudding is ready when it is excellent.
5. Could you put in the fridge until it's cold?

6. You can serve the rice pudding with extra diced mango and chopped coconut on top.

TRES LECHES CUPCAKES:

INGREDIENTS: For the Cupcakes:

- 1 1/2 cups all-purpose flour
- 1 tsp baking powder
- 1/2 tsp baking soda
- 1/4 tsp salt
- 1/2 cup unsalted butter, softened
- 1 cup granulated sugar
- 2 large eggs
- 1 tsp vanilla extract
- 1/2 cup whole milk For the Tres Leches Syrup:
- 1 can (14 oz) sweetened condensed milk
- 1 can (12 oz) evaporated milk
- 1/2 cup canned coconut milk For the Topping:
- Whipped cream
- Maraschino cherries

Instructions: For the Cupcakes:

1. Warm the oven up to 175°F (350°F). You can line a muffin tin with cupcake cups.
2. Put the all-purpose flour, baking powder, baking soda, and salt in a bowl and mix them with a whisk.

3. Put the melted unsalted butter and granulated sugar in a different bowl and mix them until they are light and fluffy.
4. Mix the butter and vanilla extract. Then, add the giant eggs. Mix everything by beating it.
5. Add the dry ingredients to the wet ingredients one at a time, mixing the whole milk between each addition. Start with the dry ingredients and end with the whole milk. Don't mix any further than that.
6. Fill each cupcake pan with an equal amount of cupcake batter.
7. After the oven is hot, bake the cupcakes for 18 to 20 minutes or until a toothpick stuck in the middle comes out clean.
8. Here are the numbers for the Tres Leches Syrup: 8. With a whisk, mix the evaporated milk, sweetened condensed milk, and canned coconut milk in a bowl.
9. Once the cupcakes are still warm but cooled, use a stick or skewer to make several holes.
10. Pour the Tres Leches syrup over each cupcake slowly so it can soak in. This step might need to be done more than once.
11. 11. Let the Tres Leches cupcakes cool down before adding the topping.
12. Put some whipped cream on each cupcake and decorate with a maraschino cherry.
13. Serve these decadent Tres Leches cupcakes and enjoy them!

MAMEY AND COCONUT CHIA PARFAIT:

INGREDIENTS:

- 1 cup mamey pulp
- 1 can (13.5 oz) coconut milk
- 1/4 cup chia seeds
- 2 tbsp honey or maple syrup
- Fresh mamey slices and shredded coconut for garnish (optional)

Instructions:

1. Blend the mamey pulp, coconut milk, and honey or maple syrup in a mixer. Mix until it's smooth.
2. Put the mamey and coconut mix into a bowl for mixing.
3. The chia seeds should be mixed in well.
4. The mixture should be put in the fridge for at least 4 hours or overnight with the lid on to let the chia seeds thicken.
5. When you're ready to serve, put the Mamey and Coconut Chia Parfait in cups or bowls and layer it up. If you want, you can add fresh mamey slices and shredded coconut in between each layer.
6. Serve this healthy and tasty dessert, and enjoy it!

CUBAN COFFEE AND CHOCOLATE FONDUE:

INGREDIENTS:

- 8 oz semisweet chocolate, chopped
- 1/2 cup heavy cream
- 1/4 cup brewed Cuban coffee (strong)
- Dippers (e.g., marshmallows, cubed pound cake, strawberries, banana slices, etc.)

Instructions:

1. Put the chopped semisweet chocolate, heavy cream, and brewed Cuban coffee in a bowl or pot in the microwave.
2. In the microwave, heat the mixture for 20 to 30 seconds, stirring until the chocolate is melted and the mixture is smooth.
3. You can also heat the mixture over low heat while stirring it until it's smooth.
4. Move the Cuban Coffee and Chocolate Fondue to a bowl or fondue pot that can hold it.
5. For a fun fondue experience, serve with a variety of dippers.

GUAVA AND CHEESE STUFFED POP TARTS:

INGREDIENTS: For the Dough:

- 2 cups all-purpose flour
- 1 tsp salt
- 1 cup unsalted butter, cold and diced
- 1/2 cup ice water For the Filling:
- 1/2 cup guava paste, diced
- 1/2 cup cream cheese, softened
- 2 tbsp granulated sugar
- 1 large egg, beaten (for egg wash)
- Powdered sugar for dusting (optional)

Instructions: For the Dough:

1. In a mixing bowl, mix the salt and all-purpose flour.
2. Put the cold, diced, unsalted butter into the bowl with the flour.
3. You can use your fingers or a pastry cutter to cut the butter into the flour until the mixture resembles big crumbs.
4. Add the ice water a tablespoon and mix the dough until it comes together.
5. Two equal pieces of dough should be made. Roll each piece into a ball and cover it with plastic wrap.
6. Before you roll out the dough, put it in the fridge for at least 30 minutes.
7. To make the filling: 7. Put the melted cream cheese, diced guava paste, and granulated sugar in a mixing bowl. Mix everything well.
8. To Put Together: 8. Warm the oven up to 190°C (375°F). Put parchment paper on the bottom of a baking sheet.

9. Put some flour on a table and roll one of the chilled dough disks into a big rectangle about 1/8 inch thick.
10. You can cut the dough into squares of any size, but most are about 3x4 inches.
11. Spoon some guava and cream cheese filling into the middle of half of the squares.
12. Beat an egg and use it to brush the sides of the filled rectangles.
13. Place another dough rectangle on top of each filled rectangle and press the sides together to seal.
14. For a pretty seal, crimp the sides with a fork.
15. Use more beaten eggs to brush the tops of the pop tarts.
16. Set the baking sheet ready and put the pop tarts on it.
17. Heat the oven and put the pop-tarts in it. Bake for 20 to 25 minutes or until the tops are golden brown.
18. Remove them from the oven and set them on a wire rack to cool.
19. Add powdered sugar on top if you like.
20. Whether they are warm or cold, serve the Guava and Cheese Stuffed Pop Tarts. Have fun!

PINEAPPLE COCONUT OATMEAL BARS:

INGREDIENTS:

- 1 1/2 cups old-fashioned oats
- 1 cup all-purpose flour
- 1/2 cup shredded coconut

- 1/2 cup granulated sugar
- 1/2 cup unsalted butter, melted
- 1 cup canned crushed pineapple, drained
- 1/4 cup canned coconut milk
- 1 large egg
- 1/2 tsp vanilla extract
- 1/4 tsp salt

Instructions:

1. Warm the oven up to 175°F (350°F). A 9x9-inch baking pan should be greased.
2. Old-fashioned oats, all-purpose flour, shredded coconut, powdered sugar, and melted unsalted butter should all be mixed in a bowl. Mix until the dough is broken up.
3. To make the crust, press half of the oat mixture into the bottom of a baking pan that has been greased.
4. Put the crushed pineapple drained, the giant egg, vanilla extract, and salt in a different bowl. Mix everything well.
5. Spread the pineapple mix on top of the oat crust in the baking pan.
6. Spread the rest of the oat mixture evenly on top of the pineapple.
7. The bars should be set, and the top should be golden brown in a hot oven after 30 to 35 minutes.
8. Remove
9. them from the oven and leave them in the pan to cool down.
10. Cut the Pineapple Coconut Oatmeal Bars into squares and serve them after cooling. Enjoy these treats with fruit and coconut!

COCONUT TIRAMISU:

INGREDIENTS:

- 1 1/2 cups heavy cream
- 1/2 cup powdered sugar
- 8 oz mascarpone cheese
- 1 cup canned coconut milk
- 1/2 cup brewed espresso or strong coffee, cooled
- 2 tbsp rum (optional)
- 1 package (7 oz) ladyfingers
- Unsweetened cocoa powder for dusting

Instructions:

1. Heavy cream and powdered sugar should be whipped together in a bowl until stiff peaks form.
2. Mascarpone cheese should be mixed in a different bowl until it is smooth.
3. Mix the mascarpone cheese and whipped cream together slowly until well blended.
4. Put the canned coconut milk, made coffee or espresso, and rum (if using) in a different bowl.
5. Do not let the ladyfingers soak too long; they should still have some structure. Quickly dip them into the coconut coffee mixture.
6. Place the soaked ladyfingers in a serving dish or individual cups. Then, add a layer of the mascarpone and whipped cream mixture on top of them.
7. Add more layers until all the ingredients are used up. Top with a layer of the mascarpone mixture to finish.

8. Put the Coconut Tiramisu in the fridge for at least two hours or until it's set.
9. To serve, sprinkle the unsweetened chocolate powder over the top.
10. Serve this tropical take on Tiramisu and enjoy it!

CARAMELIZED BANANA FOSTER:

INGREDIENTS:

- 4 ripe bananas, peeled and sliced
- 1/2 cup unsalted butter
- 1 cup brown sugar
- 1/4 cup dark rum
- 1/2 tsp ground cinnamon
- Vanilla ice cream for serving

Instructions:

1. Melt the unsalted butter over medium-low heat in a pan.
2. Slice the ripe bananas and add them to the pan. Cook for two minutes on each side until the bananas turn brown and caramelize.
3. Add the brown sugar to the bananas and mix them until the sugar is gone and the mixture starts to bubble.
4. Carefully add the dark rum to the pan, and then use a long lighter to light it. Keep your distance from the fire, and be careful.
5. Let the fires go out so the alcohol can cook off.

6. Add the ground cinnamon to the sautéed banana foster and mix it all.
7. Take it off the heat and let it cool down a bit.
8. Spread vanilla ice cream on a plate and top the caramelized banana foster with it. Enjoy this tasty treat that's on fire!

CHOCOLATE COCONUT CREAM PIE:

INGREDIENTS: For the Crust:

- 1 1/2 cups chocolate cookie crumbs
- 1/4 cup granulated sugar
- 1/2 cup unsalted butter, melted For the Filling:
- 1 1/2 cups canned coconut milk
- 1 1/2 cups whole milk
- 1/2 cup granulated sugar
- 1/4 cup cornstarch
- 4 large egg yolks
- 1/4 cup unsweetened cocoa powder
- 4 oz dark chocolate, chopped
- 2 tsp vanilla extract For the Topping:
- Sweetened whipped cream
- Shredded coconut
- Chocolate shavings

Instructions: For the Crust:

1. Mix the chocolate cookie crumbs, sugar, and melted unsalted butter in a bowl. Add more water until the mixture looks like wet sand.
2. For the crust, press the mix into a 9-inch pie dish. Hardly press it into the bottom and sides with the back of a spoon.
3. Put the crust in the fridge while you make the filling.
4. To make the filling: 4. Mix the coconut milk from a can, whole milk, sugar, cornstarch, large egg whites, and unsweetened cocoa powder in a saucepan using a whisk.
5. Place the pan on medium-low heat and stir until it gets thick and boils.
6. Take the pan off the heat and add the chopped dark chocolate and vanilla extract. Mix the ingredients until the chocolate melts and the filling is smooth.
7. Fill the pie shell with the chocolate coconut filling.
8. Put the pie in the fridge for at least four hours or until it's set.
9. Number 9 for the topping. Put sweetened whipped cream, chopped coconut, and chocolate shavings on top of the Chocolate Coconut Cream Pie before serving it.
10. Cut this rich pie into pieces and serve it!

TARO ROOT AND COCONUT MACARONS:

INGREDIENTS: For the Macarons:

- 1 3/4 cups powdered sugar
- 1 cup almond flour
- 3 large egg whites, room temperature
- 1/4 cup granulated sugar
- 1/4 cup taro root powder
- Purple food coloring (optional) For the Filling:
- 1/2 cup unsalted butter, softened
- 1 cup powdered sugar
- 2 tbsp canned coconut milk
- 1/4 cup taro root powder
- Purple food coloring (optional)

Instructions: For the Macarons:

1. Warm your oven up to 150°C/300°F. Cover two baking sheets with parchment paper.
2. Put the powdered sugar, almond flour, and taro root powder in a food processor and blend them. Blend until everything is well mixed.
3. Whip the egg whites in a bowl until they get foamy. While beating, add the white sugar little by little. Continue beating until stiff peaks form. You can add a few drops of purple food coloring if you want the color you want.
4. Carefully mix the almond flour mixture into the egg whites that have been beaten until the batter is smooth and has a ribbon texture.
5. Fill a pipe bag with a round tip with the macaron batter.
6. Leave space between each small round of batter that you pipe on the baking sheets that have been prepared.
7. Let the macarons rest for about 30 minutes or until a skin forms on top. You can do this by tapping the baking sheets on the counter to eliminate any air bubbles.

8. Place the macarons in an oven that has already been warm. Bake for 15 to 18 minutes or until they are set and have feet.
9. Remove them from the oven and leave them on the baking sheets to cool down.
10. Take 10 for the filling. Softened raw butter should be beaten in a bowl until it turns creamy.
11. Slowly add the coconut milk in a can, the taro root powder, and the purple food coloring if you want to. Beat the filling until it is smooth and the color you want.
12. To Get Together: 12. Organize the macaron pieces by size.
13. Put a little filling on the flat side of one shell and then put another shell between them.
14. Do this again with the rest of the macarons.
15. Put in the fridge for at least 24 hours to let the flavors mix.
16. When you serve the Taro Root and Coconut Macarons, enjoy the delicious taste of taro and coconut together.

GUAVA AND CREAM CHEESE STUFFED BABKA:

INGREDIENTS: For the Dough:

- 4 cups all-purpose flour
- 1/2 cup granulated sugar
- 1 packet (2 1/4 tsp) active dry yeast
- 1/2 cup whole milk

- 1/2 cup unsalted butter, softened
- 4 large eggs
- 1 tsp vanilla extract
- 1/2 tsp salt For the Filling:
- 8 oz cream cheese, softened
- 1/2 cup granulated sugar
- 1/2 cup guava paste, diced For the Streusel Topping:
- 1/4 cup all-purpose flour
- 1/4 cup granulated sugar
- 1/4 cup unsalted butter, cold and diced
- Powdered sugar for dusting (optional)

Instructions: For the Dough:

1. Put two cups of all-purpose flour, sugar, and active dry yeast in a mixing bowl.
2. Put unsalted butter and whole milk in a pot. Heat them over low heat until the butter melts. Take it off the heat and let it cool down a bit.
3. Mix the milk and butter, then add it to the bowl with the dry ingredients. Mix everything well.
4. One at a time, add the eggs and mix well after each one.
5. Add the salt and vanilla extract and mix well.
6. Slowly add the last two cups of all-purpose flour and mix the dough until it comes together.
7. For about 5 to 7 minutes, knead the dough on a floured surface until it's smooth and springy.
8. To make the dough double in size, put it in an oiled bowl and cover it with a clean cloth. Let it rise in a warm place for about an hour.

9. For the Filling: 9. Put the softened cream cheese and sugar in a bowl and mix them together until they are smooth.
10. Ten for the streusel topping. Mix the all-purpose flour, powdered sugar, and cold, diced, unsalted butter in a different bowl. With your fingers, break up the dough into small pieces.
11. To Put Together: 11. Warm your oven up to 175°F (350°F). Prepare a bread pan by greasing it.
12. Punch down the dough that has risen on a floured surface and roll it out into a square.
13. Cover the dough with the cream cheese filling.
14. Cut the guava paste and sprinkle it on the cream cheese filling.
15. Form a tight log out of the dough.
16. Put the dough log in the loaf pan that has been oiled.
17. Put the crumb topping on top of the babka.
18. Warm the oven up and put the babka in it. Bake for 45 to 50 minutes or until it turns golden brown, and when you tap it on the bottom, it sounds hollow.
19. When you remove it from the oven, let it cool in the pan for a few minutes. Then, move it to a wire rack to finish cooling.
20. Add powdered sugar on top if you like.
21. Spread the Guava and Cream Cheese Stuffed Babka on a plate and serve it. Have fun!

CUBAN COFFEE ICE CREAM SANDWICHES:

INGREDIENTS: For the Coffee Ice Cream:

- 2 cups heavy cream
- 1 cup whole milk
- 3/4 cup granulated sugar
- 1/4 cup brewed Cuban coffee (strong)
- 1 tbsp instant coffee granules
- 1 tsp vanilla extract For the Cookies:
- 2 cups all-purpose flour
- 1/2 cup unsweetened cocoa powder
- 1 tsp baking soda
- 1/2 tsp salt
- 1 cup unsalted butter, softened
- 1 1/2 cups granulated sugar
- 2 large eggs
- 1 tsp vanilla extract
- Powdered sugar for dusting (optional)

Instructions: For the Coffee Ice Cream:

1. Mix the heavy cream, whole milk, sugar, hot Cuban coffee, instant coffee granules, and vanilla extract in a bowl using a whisk until everything is well-mixed.
2. Put the coffee ice cream mix into an ice cream maker and churn it as directed by the maker's maker.
3. Put the churned ice cream in a jar that won't let air in and freeze it until it's firm.
4. To make the cookies: 4. Warm the oven up to 175°F (350°F). Put parchment paper on the bottom of a baking sheet.
5. Whisk the all-purpose flour, unsweetened cocoa powder, baking soda, and salt in a bowl.

6. Put the melted unsalted butter and granulated sugar in a different bowl and mix them until they are light and fluffy.
7. Mix the butter and vanilla extract. Then, add the giant eggs. Mix everything by beating it.
8. Slowly add the dry ingredients to the wet ones until they are mixed.
9. Place cookie dough spoonfuls on the baking sheet that has been prepared, leaving room between each one.
10. After the oven is hot, bake the cookies for 10 to 12 minutes or until set.
11. Take them out of the oven and let them cool for a few minutes on the baking sheet. Then, move them to a wire rack to cool down.
12. To Put Together: 12. Once the cookies and the coffee ice cream are cool, put a big scoop of the ice cream on the flat side of one cookie.
13. To make an ice cream sandwich, put another cookie on top.
14. Sprinkle with powdered sugar if you want to.
15. Enjoy this tasty treat after you serve the Cuban Coffee Ice Cream Sandwiches.

PINEAPPLE COCONUT CREME BRULEE:

INGREDIENTS:

- 2 cups canned coconut milk
- 1/2 cup canned crushed pineapple, drained

- 1/2 cup granulated sugar
- 6 large egg yolks
- 1 tsp vanilla extract
- 1/4 cup brown sugar (for caramelizing)

Instructions:

1. Warm the oven up to 160°C (325°F). In a serving dish, put six ramekins.
2. Put the canned coconut milk and rinsed crushed pineapple in a saucepan. Please put it on medium heat and cook it until it simmer. Take it off the heat and let it cool down a bit.
3. Add the granulated sugar, large egg whites, and vanilla extract to a mixing bowl. Use a whisk to mix the ingredients well.
4. Slowly add the warm coconut milk and pineapple mixture to the egg yolk mixture while stirring constantly.
5. Move the custard mix through a fine-mesh sieve into a clean bowl to eliminate lumps.
6. Put equal amounts of the custard mix into each of the six ramekins.
7. Put the baking dish with the ramekins in an oven that is already hot. Fill the baking dish with hot water until it comes up about halfway up the sides of the ramekins. This will make a water bath.
8. The creme brulee should be baked for 40 to 45 minutes or until it is set but still has a little give in the middle.
9. Take the ramekins out of the water and let them cool down until they are at room temperature. After that, put it in the fridge for at least 4 hours or until it's cold.
10. When ready to serve them, put a thin layer of brown sugar on top of each creme brulee.

11. Use a kitchen torch to turn the sugar into caramel until it's golden and crispy.
12. Enjoy the delicious, tropical Pineapple Coconut Creme Brulee after you serve it.

GUAVA AND CHEESE STUFFED COOKIE SANDWICHES:

INGREDIENTS: For the Cookies:

- 2 1/4 cups all-purpose flour
- 1/2 tsp baking soda
- 1 cup unsalted butter, softened
- 1/2 cup granulated sugar
- 1 cup brown sugar, packed
- 2 large eggs
- 1 tsp vanilla extract
- 1 cup chocolate chips For the Filling:
- Guava paste, diced
- Cream cheese softened

Instructions: For the Cookies:

1. Warm the oven up to 175°F (350°F). Put parchment paper on the bottom of a baking sheet.
2. Put the all-purpose flour and baking soda in a bowl and mix them together with a whisk.

3. Put the melted unsalted butter, granulated sugar, and brown sugar in a different bowl and mix them until smooth.
4. Mix the butter and vanilla extract. Then, add the giant eggs. Mix everything by beating it.
5. Slowly add the dry ingredients to the wet ones until they are mixed.
6. Add the chocolate chips and mix them in.
7. Place cookie dough spoonfuls on the baking sheet that has been prepared, leaving room between each one.
8. The cookies should be baked in an oven that is hot for 10 to 12 minutes or until golden brown.
9. Take them out of the oven and let them cool for a few minutes on the baking sheet. Then, move them to a wire rack to cool down.
10. To make the filling: 10. Spread some softened cream cheese on the flat side of one cookie after it cools down.
11. On top of the cream cheese, put diced guava paste.
12. Put another cookie on top to make a sandwich.
13. Please do it again with the rest of the cookies.
14. You can enjoy these Guava and Cheese Stuffed Cookie Sandwiches after you serve them.

COCONUT KEY LIME TARTLETS:

INGREDIENTS: For the Tartlet Crust:

- 1 1/4 cups all-purpose flour
- 1/4 cup granulated sugar

- 1/4 tsp salt
- 1/2 cup unsalted butter, cold and diced
- 1 large egg yolk
- 2 tbsp ice water For the Filling:
- 3 large egg yolks
- 1 can (14 oz) sweetened condensed milk
- 1/2 cup canned coconut milk
- Zest of 3-4 key limes
- 1/2 cup fresh key lime juice (or regular lime juice)
- Whipped cream for topping
- Lime zest for garnish

Instructions: For the Tartlet Crust:

1. Mix the all-purpose flour, sugar, and salt in a food blender.
2. Add the cold, diced butter that doesn't have salt to the food processor. Pulse the ingredients together until they look like big crumbs.
3. Mix the big egg yolk and ice water in a small bowl using a whisk.
4. Slowly pour the egg yolk mixture into the food processor and pulse until the dough forms.
5. Spread the dough on a floured surface and make a disk with it.
6. For at least 30 minutes, put the dough in the fridge while it's wrapped in plastic.
7. Warm the oven up to 175°F (350°F). Put some butter in a tartlet or small muffin tin.
8. Roll out the cold dough on a floured surface until it is about 1/8 inch thick.

9. To make the tartlet shells, cut out small dough rings and press them into a tartlet pan or cupcake tin.
10. Use a fork to make holes in the bottom of the tartlet shells.
11. The tartlet shells should be baked in a hot oven for 10 to 12 minutes or until golden brown.
12. Remove them from the oven and leave them in the pan to cool down.
13. To make the filling: 13. The big egg whites, sweetened condensed milk, canned coconut milk, key lime zest, and fresh key lime juice should all be mixed well in a bowl.
14. After the shells have cooled, put the key lime filling inside them.
15. Put it in an already hot oven and bake for 10 to 12 minutes or until the filling is set.
16. Take the tartlets out of the oven and let them cool to room temperature before putting them in the fridge.
17. Put the Coconut Key Lime Tartlets in the fridge, and then add whipped cream and more lime juice on top.
18. Serve these tasty tarts and enjoy them!

TRES LECHES TIRAMISU TRIFLES:

INGREDIENTS: For the Tres Leches Soaking Liquid:

- 1 can (14 oz) sweetened condensed milk
- 1 can (12 oz) evaporated milk
- 1/2 cup canned coconut milk

- 2 tbsp brewed espresso or strong coffee, cooled For the Tiramisu Filling:
- 1 1/2 cups mascarpone cheese
- 1/2 cup powdered sugar
- 2 tsp vanilla extract
- 1/4 cup brewed espresso or strong coffee, cooled
- Ladyfingers
- Unsweetened cocoa powder for dusting
- Chocolate shavings for garnish (optional)

Instructions: For the Tres Leches Soaking Liquid:

1. Add the evaporated milk, canned coconut milk, sweetened condensed milk, and made espresso or coffee to a mixing bowl. Use a whisk to mix the ingredients well.
2. To fill the Tiramisu: To make the mascarpone cheese smooth and creamy, put it in a different bowl and whisk in the powdered sugar, vanilla extract, and hot coffee or espresso.
3. To Put Together the Trifles: 3. Put ladyfingers on the bottom of serving glasses or individual trifle plates.
4. The ladyfingers should be soaked, but not too much. Drizzle them with the Tres Leches soaking juice.
5. Put some of the Tiramisu filling on top of the wet ladyfingers.
6. Put more layers on top of each other, ending with a layer of the Tiramisu filling.
7. Sprinkle unsweetened cocoa powder on top, and if you want, you can add chocolate pieces as a decoration.
8. Put the Tres Leches Tiramisu Trifles in the fridge for at least 4 hours or until they are set.
9. Serve this mix of Tres Leches and Tiramisu tastes, and enjoy it!

CONCLUSION

This is the end of our cooking tour through this Cuba dessert cookbook. We hope you enjoyed every minute of learning about the delicious world of Cuban sweets. From the first page, we were taken on a journey to discover the many delicious desserts that make up this beautiful Caribbean island's sweet fabric. Before we say goodbye, remember the fun times, tastes, and stories that have helped us learn more about Cuba's dessert culture.

In these pages, you've learned that Cuban desserts are more than just delicious treats; they also reflect the country's history, tradition, and strength. Each treat shows how Cuban identity comprises different cultures coming together. Pastries and flan were brought to Cuba by the Spanish, and African, Chinese, and Indigenous people changed traditional recipes in their own unique ways.

In the cozy warmth of a Cuban kitchen, we've seen how hardworking and creative home bakers are as they turn simple ingredients into delicious works of art. We now know that it's not just the dish itself that matters but also the love and care that went into making it. We've come to believe that cake is more than just a sweet treat; it's a way to celebrate life, family, and community.

When you use the recipes and tips you've learned here in your home, remember that you're not just making Cuban desserts again; you're also passing on a piece of Cuban history, culture, and tradition. You connect with Cuba's heart and soul when you make a traditional Cuban Flan for a special event or enjoy Churros and Chocolate on a cold night.

If you want to learn more about Cuban desserts, feel free to keep trying new tastes and sharing your delicious creations with your family and friends. In the same way that the people of Cuba have shared their sweet customs with us, you can now do the same for future generations.

Thank you for coming with us on this fantastic trip through food and culture. As you enjoy each bite, may it be a sweet reminder of Cuba's lively energy, strength, and friendliness. Until we meet again, "Hasta luego," and may the sweet sounds of Cuba always fill your home.

The End